A PHOTOGRAPHIC ATLAS OF SHARK ANATOMY

THE GROSS MORPHOLOGY OF *Squalus acanthias*

A PHOTOGRAPHIC ATLAS
OF SHARK ANATOMY

THE GROSS MORPHOLOGY OF *SQUALUS ACANTHIAS*

CARL GANS   THOMAS S. PARSONS

The University of Chicago Press
Chicago and London

The University of Chicago Press, Chicago 60637
The University of Chicago Press, Ltd., London

University of Chicago Press edition 1981
Printed in the United States of America
96 95 94 93 92 91 90 89 88 87   6 5 4 3 2

Library of Congress Cataloging in Publication Data

Gans, Carl, 1923—
   A photographic atlas of shark anatomy.

   Reprint of the 1964 ed. published by Academic
Press, New York.
   Bibliography: p.
   Includes index.
   1. Squalus acanthias—Anatomy—Laboratory manuals.
2. Fishes—Anatomy—Laboratory manuals. 3. Dissection.
I. Parsons, Thomas Sturges, 1930– joint author.
II. Title.
QL813.F57G36 1981– 597′.31 80–24528
ISBN 0–226–28120–5 (pbk.)

CONTENTS

INTRODUCTION

The spiny dogfish, *Squalus acanthias* Linné, is one of the most widely used animals in comparative anatomy laboratories. The present atlas of photographs provides a detailed visual guide to the morphology of this common form.

Dissection of anatomical structures is a necessity for true comprehension of regional topography. Since the student ordinarily has only one specimen and even careful dissection implies displacement and destruction, this atlas has been planned to facilitate visual recall of the original condition. The basic intent is to furnish a rapid guide to the location and general appearance of some 500 structures. It therefore demonstrates anatomical detail by labeled photographs and, where necessary, additional explanatory drawings.

The atlas is not intended as a substitute for a dissection guide, but as a supplement to a course of dissection. Therefore, the text, confined to a few explanatory comments opposite each page, has been reduced to a minimum. Its purpose is to call attention to points which, though illustrated, are often missed by students. Mention is also made of special problems in anatomical terminology. Embryological and histological material has, however, been omitted.

Not all specimens are exactly alike. Sexual dimorphism affects overall size and shape of the body and the pelvic fins, as well as the gonads and other parts of the genital system. In addition there are frequent variations in other structures, especially in the circulatory system. Thus, although major anomalies have been avoided in the photographs, the latter cannot be expected to correspond perfectly to any particular specimen used in the laboratory.

The comprehension of topography has been facilitated by illustrating various dissections and sections not commonly utilized or shown in manuals. It is hoped that they will enhance the utility of the atlas to the student, to the laboratory instructor, and to any others who may desire a guide to the morphology of this species.

We have in general maintained the convention that the specimen's head should point to the top or left of the plate. The views follow anatomical terminology; they thus indicate the position of the viewer, i.e. a posterior view looks forward and an anterior view backward, and so forth. In most cases the photographs show more structures than are labeled so as not to obscure them with too many leaders. Ordinarily leaders with arrows indicate structural details, while those without denote regions.

All of the dissections were made on standard, commercially available dogfish, generally with the arterial and hepatic portal systems injected. They were done as carefully as possible, for the most part, under a dissecting microscope. In some cases dissections were carried out on frozen material, were treated with such stains as eosin, toluidine blue, and hematoxylin, or were slightly etched with sodium hypochlorite to bring out details; such cases are usually mentioned in the descriptions of the individual photographs. The sections were cut from deep-frozen specimens using either a hand-held microtome blade or a band-saw. All of the photographs were made with a single lens reflex 35-mm camera equipped with an $f2.8$ Tessar lens and various filters. Standard photographic materials and techniques were used.

All photographs feature *Squalus acanthias* and the comments are based entirely on that species. Other small elasmobranchs are occasionally dissected; in some countries they are commonly used. Differences may be expected, and their degree will depend upon the relationship of the species used. An estimate of the degree of difference may be obtained by reference to Bigelow and Schroeder's monograph (1948). This volume also lists the various synonyms for *Squalus acanthias* (*Acanthias vulgaris* and *Squalus suckleyi* occur most often in the older anatomical literature), and furnishes a mine of information on sharks in general.

Lack of a single accepted anatomical terminology is another problem that had to be overcome. There is considerable variation in different laboratory manuals and texts. We have checked for, and listed in the index, all anatomical names and synonyms used in approximately two dozen commonly used texts, manuals, and important papers. This does not exhaust the possible synonyms by any means, but the list should include most of the names that are apt to be encountered. Where we found that a single name had been used by different authors for two different structures, we have listed the name twice and left it to the reader to determine the application of the name he is actually seeking. The synonyms refer to the names adopted by us. The latter are the only terms that are used in plate captions and labels.

Although the choice of terms naturally reflects our preferences, this is not primarily a terminological study; no attempt has been made to check all the latest information concerning views on homologies and other such considerations. We also disclaim any responsibility for the inappropriateness of many of the synonyms and merely list what we have found. Names and synonyms are listed only for those structures which are figured or discussed in this atlas; there are, of course, many others which we have omitted.

Although there are a few terms given in Latin, we have, as far as possible, used English equivalents. Thus for terms such as Arteria femoralis, Musculus spiracularis, Nervus olfactorius, and Vena renalis, refer to Femoral artery, Spiracular muscle, Olfactory nerve, Renal vein, and so on. Compound names are listed only once and are alphabetized by the first word in the usual order. Thus Anterior cardinal vein is listed under the letter A. Right and left are not used in the index although they may appear in figure captions.

Throughout the index, the terms which we have used in plate captions or the text are given in bold-face type while the synonyms appear in light-face type. The latter are followed, after an equal sign, by the term which we have used for the structure in question. The entries in bold-face type are followed by the plate and then the label number separated by a hyphen (e.g. 35-19); where mention is in the comments, a C appears instead of the label number (e.g. 35-C), and mention in the title of a plate is designated similarly by a T.

Attention should be called to a few major works on dogfish anatomy; students desiring further references are directed to the often extensive bibliographies in these studies. An especially valuable volume is that of Daniel (1934). It deals mostly with *Heptanchus,* but all elasmobranchs are well treated. A more recent and splendidly illustrated work is that of Marinelli and Strenger (1959). The basic sources on the structure of the circulatory system and of the cranial nerves, both of which loom large in any dissection program, are O'Donoghue and Abbott (1928) and Norris and Hughes (1920) respectively and we have generally followed their terminology. Finally two great reference works may be noted: Bolk *et al.* (1931-1939), which still remains the most important compendium on comparative vertebrate anatomy; and Grassé (1958), which presents a mass of information on all aspects of the biology of fishes.

While all the dissections and photographs were made by the authors, we are indebted to several people for their assistance in the preparation of this atlas: Miss Charlyn Rhodes who provided technical assistance, Dr. Virginia Cummings and Dr. Margaret C. Parsons who drew the sketches, Mrs. K. A. Gans who did much of the typing, and Dr. John F. Storr for help and advice. We also wish to thank General Biological Supply House, Incorporated, which supplied a few dogfish used in the dissections, and Ward's Natural Science Establishment, Incorporated, which allowed us to photograph and donated some of their skeletal preparations. Finally we should like to express our appreciation to Dr. Ernest E. Williams without whose encouragement we would never have undertaken the preparation of this atlas.

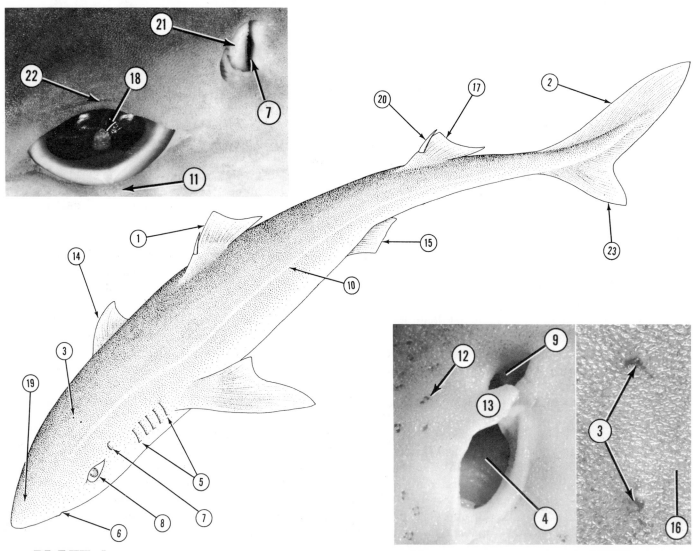

PLATE 1 EXTERNAL FEATURES A. Whole animal (center); B. Eye and spiracle (top left); C. External naris (bottom center); D. Endolymphatic pores (bottom right).

LABELS

1. Anterior dorsal fin
2. Dorsal lobe of Caudal fin
3. Endolymphatic pores
4. Excurrent aperture of naris
5. External gill slits
6. External naris
7. External spiracular pore
8. Eye
9. Incurrent aperture of naris
10. Lateral line
11. Lower eyelid
12. Mucous pores of Ampullae of Lorenzini
13. Nasal flap
14. Pectoral fin
15. Pelvic fin
16. Placoid scales
17. Posterior dorsal fin
18. Pupil
19. Snout
20. Spine of dorsal fin
21. Spiracular valve with Pseudobranch on posterior wall
22. Upper eyelid
23. Ventral lobe of Caudal fin

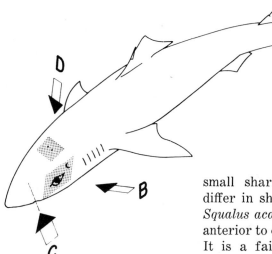

COMMENTS

The different small sharks occasionally dissected differ in shape and fin arrangement. *Squalus acanthias* always has a spine anterior to each of the two dorsal fins. It is a fairly rigid, free-swimming carnivore, showing little differentiation of the body into head, trunk, and tail.

As in all Chondrichthyes this species possesses numerous placoid scales (or dermal denticles). Their size, shape, and arrangement may vary between species and, within a given species, both regionally and ontogenetically (Sayles and Hershkowitz, 1937).

PLATE 1 / 5

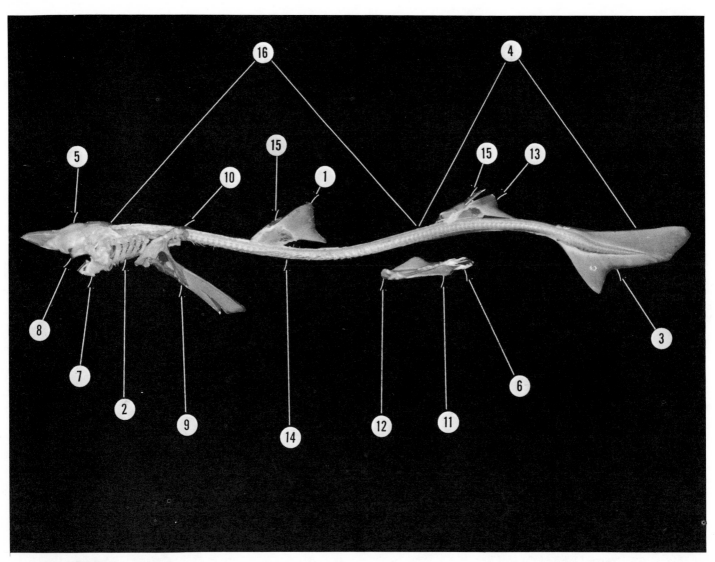

PLATE 2 SKELETON

LABELS

1. Anterior dorsal fin
2. Branchial arch
3. Caudal fin
4. Caudal vertebrae
5. Chondrocranium
6. Clasper
7. Meckel's carlilage
8. Palatoquadrate
9. Pectoral fin
10. Pectoral girdle
    (Scapular process)
11. Pelvic fin
12. Pelvic girdle
13. Posterior dorsal fin
14. Rib
15. Spine of dorsal fin
16. Trunk vertebrae

COMMENTS

The endoskeleton of Chondrichthyes is composed entirely of cartilage. Most of this is hyaline, but some is fibrous. In *Squalus* only elements of the vertebral column calcify to a noticeable extent, but in many of the larger species cartilage calcification is far more extensive.

The pectoral girdle lies in immediate juxtaposition to the vertebral column, while the pelvic girdle is connected to the column only via the axial musculature.

This photograph is of a wet-mounted skeleton. *In situ* the vertebral column would be straight, not sway backed.

PLATE 2 / 7

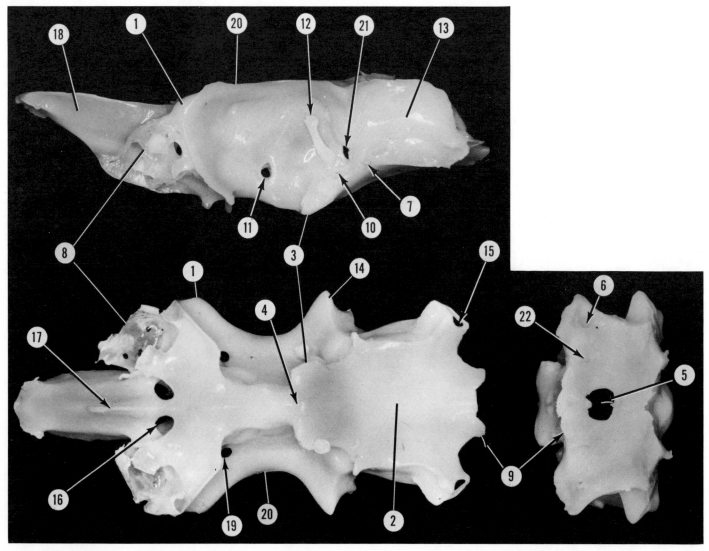

PLATE 3 CHONDROCRANIUM   A. Lateral view (top); B. Ventral view (bottom left); C. Posterior view (bottom right).

LABELS

1. Antorbital process
2. Basal plate
3. Basitrabecular process
4. Carotid foramen
5. Foramen magnum
6. Glossopharyngeal foramen
7. Hyomandibular foramen
8. Nasal capsule
9. Occipital condyle
10. Optic artery canal
11. Optic foramen
12. Optic pedicel
13. Otic capsule
14. Postorbital process
15. Postotic fenestra in Postotic process
16. Rostral fenestra
17. Rostral keel
18. Rostrum
19. Superficial ophthalmic foramen
20. Supraorbital crest
21. Trigemino-facial foramen
22. Vagus foramen

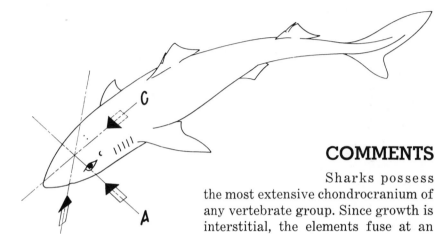

COMMENTS

Sharks possess the most extensive chondrocranium of any vertebrate group. Since growth is interstitial, the elements fuse at an early age and continue growing; the adult chondrocranium thus shows no sutures.

Most of these and the succeeding skull preparations were made from brine-preserved specimens. Terminal structures, particularly when thin, such as the nasal capsules, are often damaged, since the tensile strength of cartilage is much less than that of the surrounding tissue. Cleaning is often less than perfect (as in Plates 4 and 5). Some connective tissue has been retained to maintain the articulation of the discrete cartilages.

PLATE 3 / 9

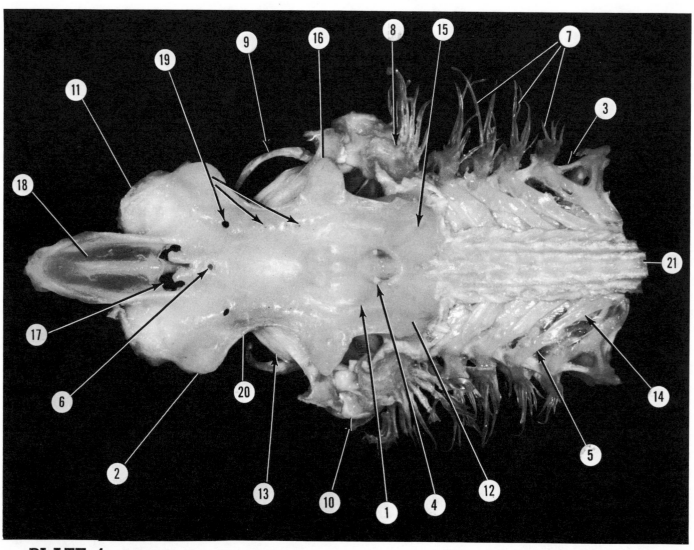

PLATE 4 ANTERIOR SKELETON—Dorsal View

LABELS

1. Anterior vertical semicircular canal (within cartilage)
2. Antorbital process
3. Connective tissue remnants
4. Endolymphatic foramen in Endolymphatic fossa
5. Epibranchial
6. Epiphyseal foramen
7. Gill rays
8. Hyomandibular
9. Labial cartilage
10. Meckel's cartilage
11. Nasal capsule
12. Otic capsule
13. Palatoquadrate
14. Pharyngobranchial
15. Posterior vertical semicircular canal (within cartilage)
16. Postorbital process
17. Rostral fenestra
18. Rostrum
19. Superficial ophthalmic foramina
20. Supraorbital crest
21. Trunk vertebra

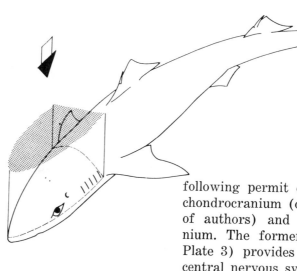

COMMENTS

This plate and the following permit comparison of the chondrocranium (or "neurocranium" of authors) and the splanchnocranium. The former (also shown in Plate 3) provides a capsule for the central nervous system and anterior sense organs. The latter forms the skeleton of the jaws and gills.

Two structures clearly shown but difficult to label are the precerebral cavity, the depression within the rostrum, and the precerebral fenestra, the large opening between this and the cranial cavity.

The dorsal and ventral extrabranchial cartilages (shown on Plate 14) are omitted here and on Plate 5. They lie freely in the soft tissues lateral to the gill rays.

PLATE 4 / 11

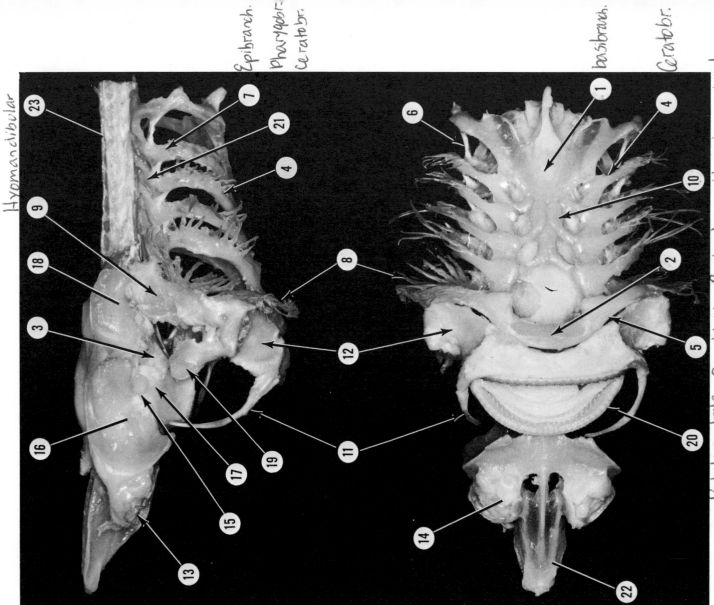

Hyomandibular

Epibranch.
Pharyngobr.
Ceratobr.

basibranch.
Ceratobr.

Palato quadrate Ceratohyal Basihyal Hypobranchial
ANTERIOR SKELETON   A. Lateral view (top); B. Ventral view (bottom).

PLATE 5

LABELS

1. Basibranchial
2. Basihyal
3. Basitrabecular process
4. Ceratobranchial
5. Ceratohyal
6. Connective tissue
7. Epibranchial
8. Gill rays
9. Hyomandibular
10. Hypobranchial
11. Labial cartilage
12. Meckel's cartilage
13. Narial aperture
14. Nasal capsule
15. Optic pedicel
16. Orbit
17. Orbital process of Palatoquadrate
18. Otic capsule
19. Otic process
20. Palatoquadrate (with Teeth)
21. Pharyngobranchial
22. Rostrum
23. Trunk vertebrae

COMMENTS

There is an extensive literature regarding the relation of visceral to somatic segmentation. Part of the problem deals with the former existence of premandibular visceral arches. Thus there has been much debate concerning the numbering of the arches. To avoid this issue we have used the terms "mandibular arch" for the jaws, "hyoid arch" for the one following it, and "branchial arches" for the most posterior ones. The embryology of these structures has most recently been discussed by El-Toubi (1949, 1952).

Note that only the three middle branchial arches have hypobranchial elements.

PLATE 5 / 13

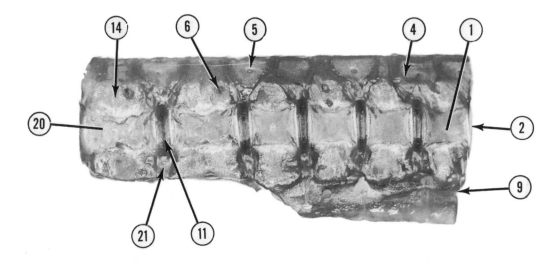

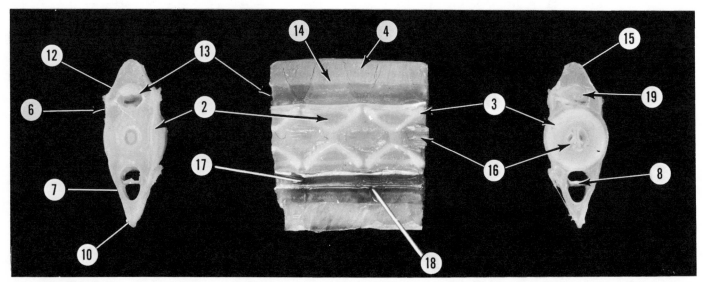

PLATE 6 VERTEBRAE A. Trunk and caudal vertebrae, lateral view (top); B. Caudal vertebra, tranverse section through a centrum (bottom left); C. Caudal vertebrae, sagittal section (bottom center); D. Caudal vertebra, transverse section between centra (bottom right).

LABELS

1. Caudal vertebra
2. Centrum
3. Corpus calcareum vertebrae
4. Dorsal intercalary plate
5. Foramen for Dorsal root of Spinal nerve
6. Foramen for Ventral root of Spinal nerve
7. Haemal arch
8. Haemal canal (partition in)
9. Haemal plate
10. Haemal spine
11. Intervertebral ligament
12. Neural arch
13. Neural canal
14. Neural plate
15. Neural spine
16. Notochordal remnant
17. Pin through foramen for branch of Caudal artery
18. Pin through foramen for branch of Caudal vein
19. Spinal cord
20. Trunk vertebra
21. Ventral intercalary plate

COMMENTS

The vertebral column changes markedly only in the region of the cloaca. Elements posterior to this (caudal vertebrae) possess haemal arches enclosing a canal for the caudal artery and vein. Anteriorly to this the trunk vertebrae lack haemal arches.

Dogfish vertebrae have long been used as an example of a primitive type, Williams (1959) has recently discussed this.

The four types of plates are discrete cartilaginous elements, while the terms arch and spine refer to topographic regions.

PLATE 6 / 15

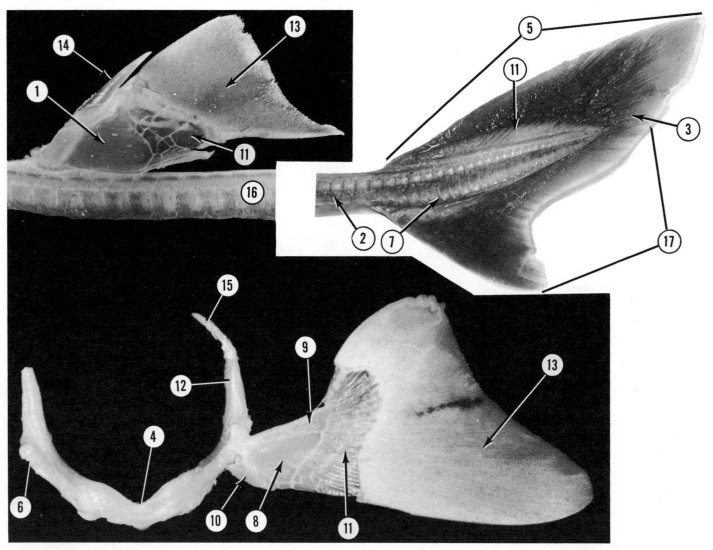

PLATE 7 FIN SKELETONS A. Anterior dorsal fin (top left); **B.** **C**audal fin (top right); C. Pectoral fin and girdle (bottom).

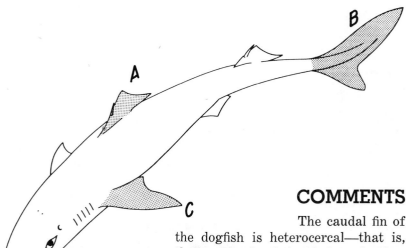

LABELS

1. Basal pterygiophore
2. Caudal vertebra
3. Ceratotrichia
4. Coracoid bar
5. Dorsal lobe of Caudal fin
6. Glenoid surface
7. Haemal arch
8. Mesopterygium
9. Metapterygium
10. Propterygium
11. Radial pterygiophore
12. Scapular process
13. Skin
14. Spine of dorsal fin
15. Suprascapular cartilage
16. Trunk vertebra
17. Ventral lobe of Caudal fin

COMMENTS

The caudal fin of the dogfish is heterocercal—that is, the vertebral axis bends into the dorsal half of the fin. The boundary between dorsal and ventral lobes can then be defined either by the obvious lobation or in reference to the vertebral axis.

The ceratotrichia are elastoid and neither horny nor cartilaginous. They form part of the integumentary system rather than the endoskeleton (Bertin, *in* Grassé, 1958, Vol. 13, Pt. 1, p. 731).

Only the anterior dorsal fin is figured on this plate; the posterior shows only minor differences from this (see Plate 2).

PLATE 7 / 17

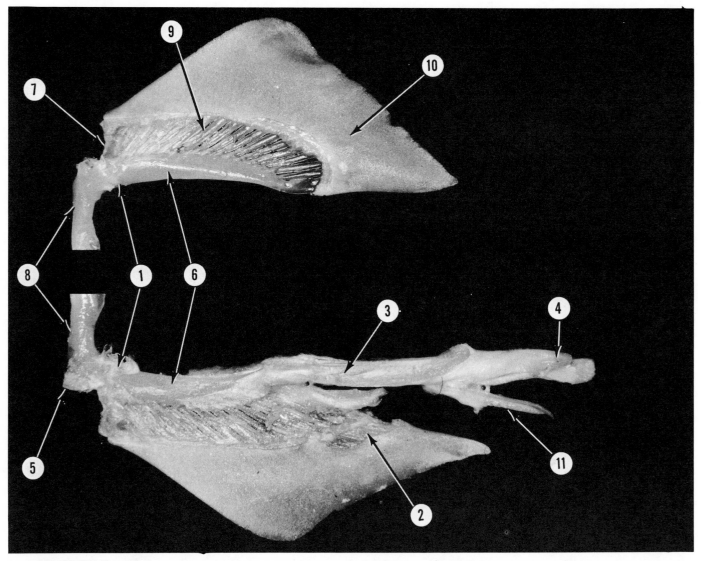

PLATE 8 PELVIC FINS A. Female pelvic fin (top); B. Male pelvic fin (bottom).

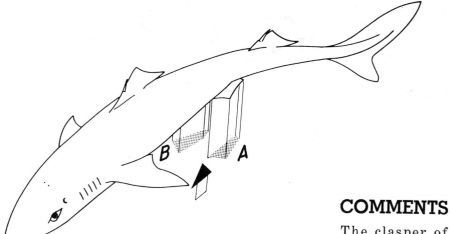

LABELS

1. Acetabular surface
2. Ceratotrichia
3. Clasper
4. Hook of Clasper
5. Iliac process
6. Metapterygium
7. Propterygium
8. Pubo-ischiadic bar
9. Radial pterygiophore
10. Skin
11. Spine of Clasper

COMMENTS

The clasper of *Squalus* is a complex organ, characteristic of male Chondrichthyes, and used for the intromission of sperm into the cloaca of the female. It is not usually dissected in detail. We recommend pretreatment in toluidine blue and differentiation in absolute alcohol for study of the individual cartilages in greater detail. This method was used on some of the preparations shown on Plates 6 and 7.

PLATE 8 / 19

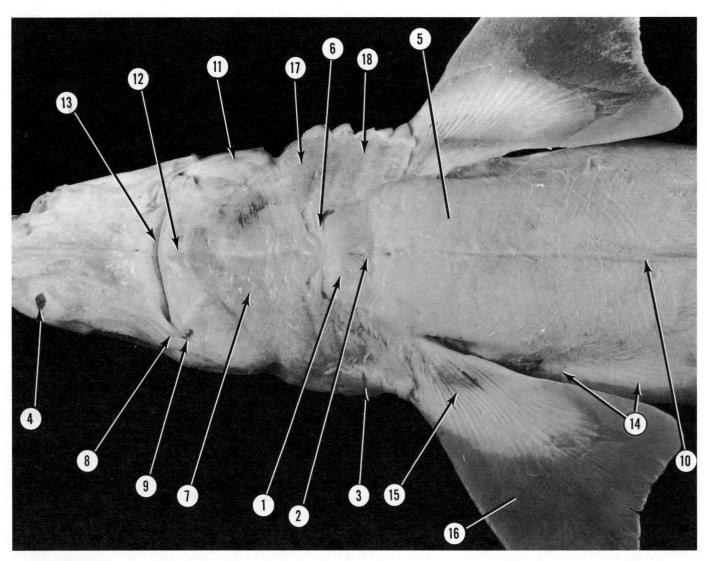

PLATE 9 SUPERFICIAL MUSCLES—Ventral view

LABELS

1. Common coracoarcual muscle
2. Coracoid bar (exposure)
3. External gill slit
4. External naris
5. Hypaxial musculature
6. Interhyoid muscle
7. Intermandibular muscle
8. Labial fold
9. Labial pocket
10. Linea alba
11. Mandibular adductor muscle
12. Meckel's cartilage
13. Mouth
14. Myocommata
15. Pectoral depressor muscle
16. Pectoral fin
17. Ventral hyoid constrictor muscle
18. Ventral superficial constrictor muscle

COMMENTS

The musculature of the gill region is extremely complex, consisting of a mixture of axial and branchial muscles with different types of embryological origin and innervation. Ventrally the true axial (hypobranchial) muscles lie deep to the branchial musculature.

It is interesting to note that the eye muscles and the preorbital muscle are the only muscles found anterior to the palatoquadrate.

The right side of the photograph demonstrates the fiber pattern of the subcutaneous fascia. These fibers connect the myocommata and generally run at nearly right angles to the underlying muscle bundles and their fibers.

PLATE 9 / 21

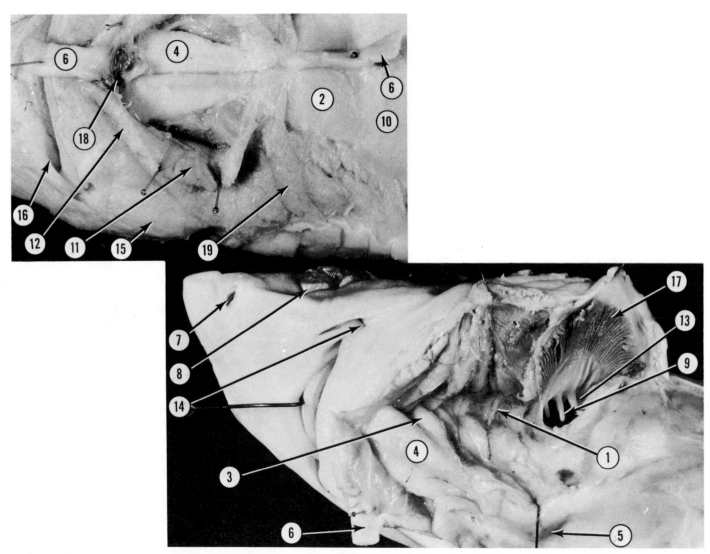

PLATE 10 HYPOBRANCHIAL MUSCULATURE A. Superficial (top); B. Deep (bottom).

LABELS

1. Afferent branchial artery
2. Common coracoarcual muscle
3. Coracobranchial muscle
4. Coracohyoid muscle
5. Coracoid bar
6. Coracomandibular muscle
7. External naris
8. Eye
9. Gill raker
10. Hypaxial musculature
11. Interhyoid muscle
12. Intermandibular muscle
13. Internal gill slit
14. Labial pocket
15. Mandibular adductor muscle
16. Mouth
17. Primary lamellae of gill
18. Thyroid gland
19. Ventral superficial constrictor muscle

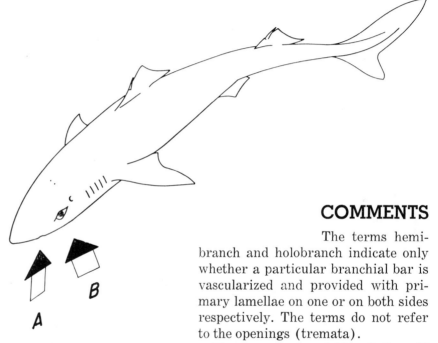

COMMENTS

The terms hemibranch and holobranch indicate only whether a particular branchial bar is vascularized and provided with primary lamellae on one or on both sides respectively. The terms do not refer to the openings (tremata).

The conspicuous folds of the gill surface are termed primary lamellae; gill filaments are secondary ridges on these.

PLATE 10 / 23

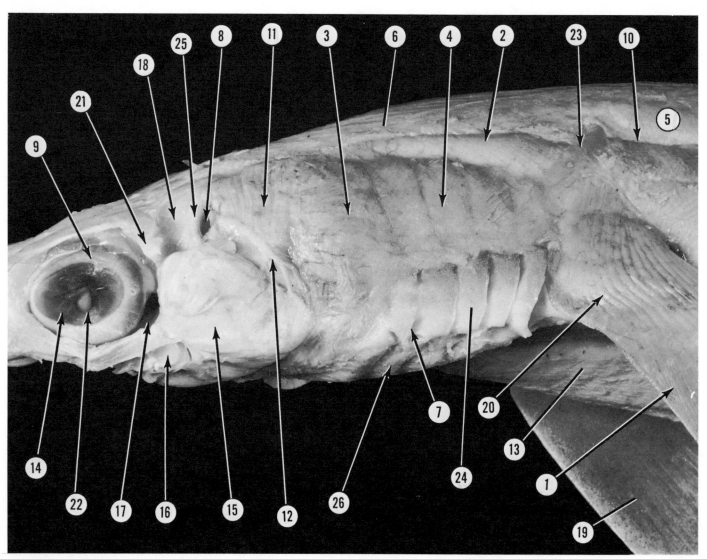

PLATE 11 MUSCLES OF HEAD AND PHARYNX—Lateral view

LABELS

1. Ceratotrichia
2. Cucullaris muscle
3. Dorsal hyoid constrictor muscle
4. Dorsal superficial constrictor muscle
5. Epaxial musculature
6. Epibranchial musculature
7. External gill slit
8. External spiracular pore
9. Eye
10. Horizontal skeletogenous septum
11. Hyomandibular levator muscle
12. Hyomandibular trunk of Facial nerve
13. Hypaxial musculature
14. Iris beneath transparent Cornea
15. Mandibular adductor muscle
16. Meckel's cartilage
17. Orbital sinus
18. Palatoquadrate levator muscle
19. Pectoral fin
20. Pectoral levator muscle
21. Postorbital process of Chondrocranium
22. Pupil
23. Scapular process
24. Skin
25. Spiracular muscle
26. Ventral superficial constrictor muscle

COMMENTS

This plate shows that the fin muscles are derivatives of the hypaxial musculature. It (and a comparison with Plate 13) further suggests the minor volumetric importance of the appendicular muscles; the much more extensive axial musculature provides the main locomotor power.

PLATE 11 / 25

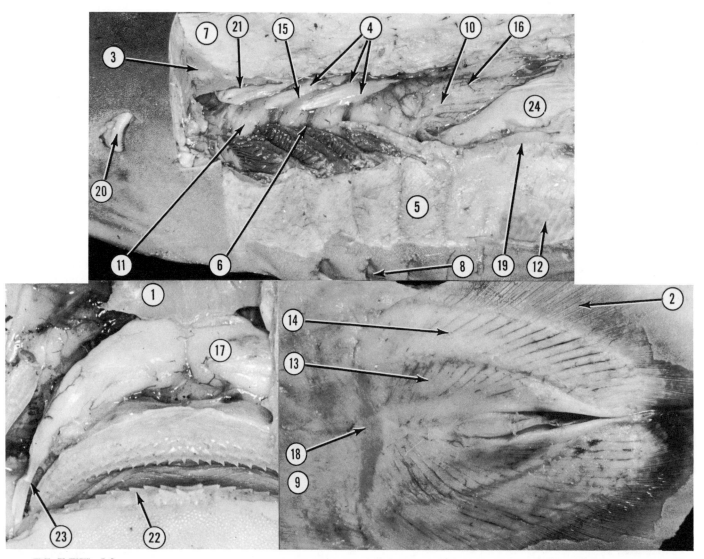

PLATE 12 MUSCLE DETAILS   A. Interarcual muscles, male (top); B. Preorbital muscle (bottom left); C. Muscles of pelvic fin, female (bottom right).

LABELS

1. Bottom of chondrocranium
2. Ceratotrichia
3. Chondrocranium
4. Dorsal interarcual muscles
5. Dorsal superficial constrictor muscle
6. Epibranchial artery
7. Epibranchial musculature
8. External gill slit
9. Hypaxial musculature
10. Intestino-accessory branch of Vagus nerve on surface of Esophageal constrictor muscle
11. Lateral interarcual muscle
12. Pectoral levator muscle
13. Pelvic adductor muscle
14. Pelvic depressor muscle
15. Pharyngobranchial
16. Posterior esophageal artery (branch of)
17. Preorbital muscle
18. Pubo-ischiadic bar (exposure)
19. Scapular process (sectioned)
20. Spiracular valve with Pseudobranch on posterior surface
21. Subspinal muscle
22. Teeth (note asymmetry)
23. Tendon of Preorbital muscle (cut)
24. Testis

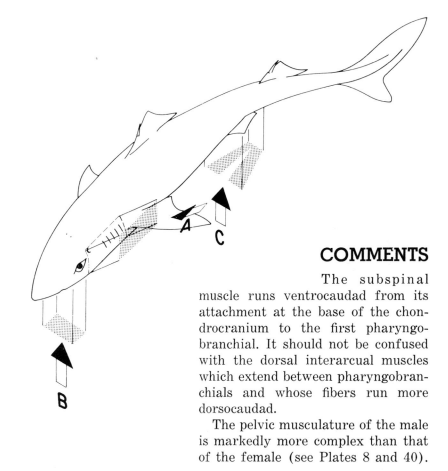

COMMENTS

The subspinal muscle runs ventrocaudad from its attachment at the base of the chondrocranium to the first pharyngobranchial. It should not be confused with the dorsal interarcual muscles which extend between pharyngobranchials and whose fibers run more dorsocaudad.

The pelvic musculature of the male is markedly more complex than that of the female (see Plates 8 and 40).

PLATE 12 / 27

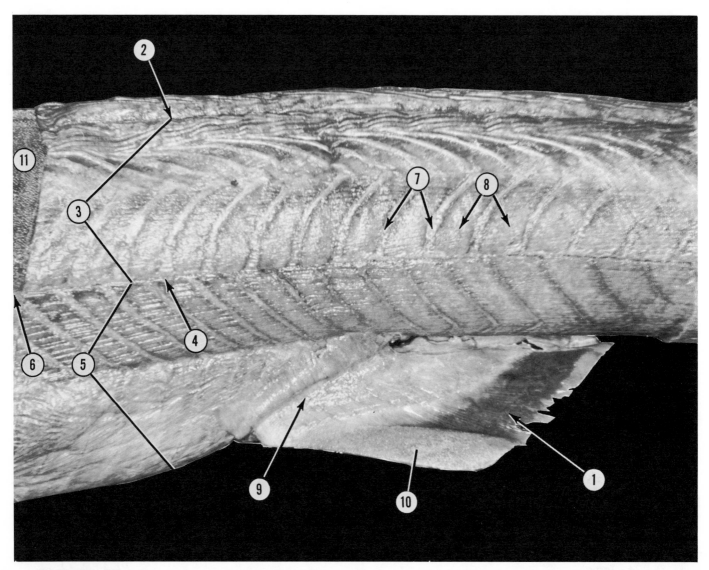

PLATE 13 BODY MUSCULATURE—Female

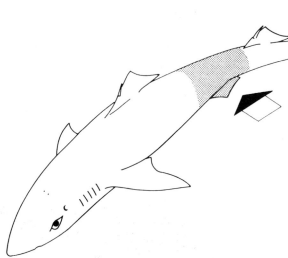

COMMENTS

This preparation has been treated to emphasize the direction of the myocommata, as well as the fiber direction in the intermediate myomeres. The technique involved removal of subcutaneous fascia, preliminary dehydration, etching with sodium hypochlorite, and differential staining with hematoxylin and eosin.

The horizontal skeletogenous septum forms the fundamental interruption of the axial musculature as demonstrated by the evident non-alignment of myocommata. The bending of the myocommata, which is presumably of great functional importance (Willemse, 1959), permits further subdivision of the axial muscles. Three dorsal, one lateral, and one ventral longitudinal bundles are recognized by some authors. The horizontal skeletogenous septum thus separates the dorsal and lateral longitudinal bundles.

LABELS

1. Ceratotrichia
2. Dorsal skeletogenous septum
3. Epaxial musculature
4. Horizontal skeletogenous septum
5. Hypaxial musculature
6. Lateral line
7. Myocommata
8. Myomeres
9. Pelvic abductor muscle
10. Pelvic fin
11. Skin

PLATE 13 / 29

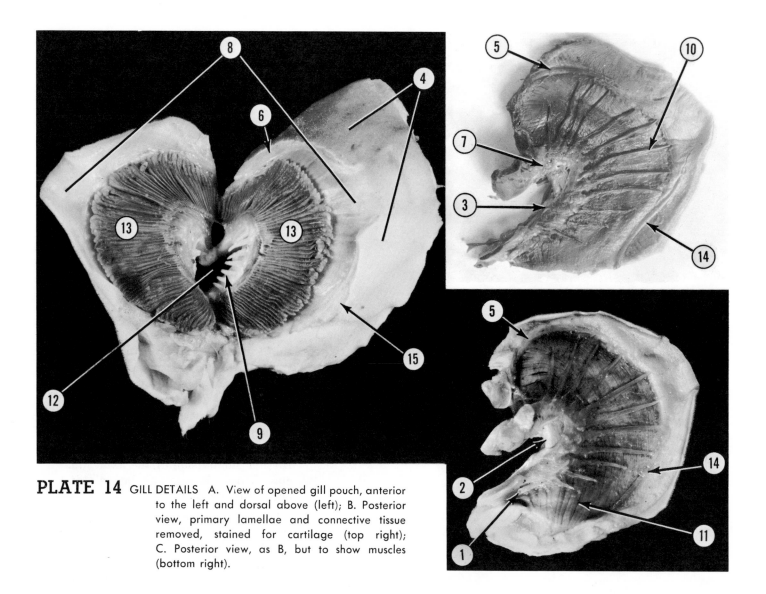

PLATE 14 GILL DETAILS A. View of opened gill pouch, anterior to the left and dorsal above (left); B. Posterior view, primary lamellae and connective tissue removed, stained for cartilage (top right); C. Posterior view, as B, but to show muscles (bottom right).

LABELS

1. Afferent branchial artery
2. Branchial adductor muscle
3. Ceratobranchial
4. Dorsal countershading
5. Dorsal extrabranchial cartilage
6. Dorsal superficial constrictor muscle
7. Epibranchial
8. External gill slit (opened)
9. Gill raker
10. Gill ray
11. Interbranchial muscle
12. Internal gill slit
13. Primary lamellae
14. Ventral extrabranchial cartilage
15. Ventral superficial constrictor muscle

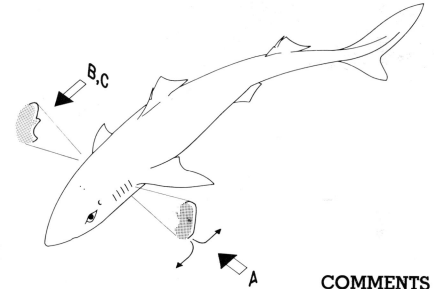

COMMENTS

There is great variation in the names applied to gill structures. In this atlas, "branchial bar" refers to everything between adjacent gill pouches, "branchial arch" is used only for the skeletal elements, and "interbranchial septum" refers to the soft parts of the bar except for the primary lamellae.

PLATE 14 / 31

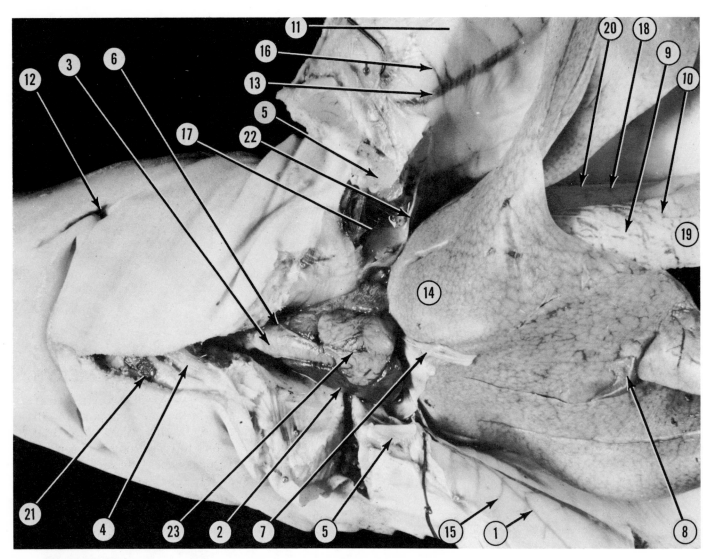

PLATE 15 ANTERIOR VISCERA—Male

LABELS

1. Anterior epigastric artery
2. Atrium
3. Conus arteriosus
4. Coracohyoid muscle
5. Coracoid bar
6. Coronary artery
7. Falciform ligament continuing dorsad into Coronary ligament
8. Gall bladder
9. Gastric artery (branches)
10. Gastric vein (branches)
11. Hypaxial musculature
12. Labial pocket
13. Lateral abdominal vein
14. Liver
15. Parietal artery
16. Parietal vein
17. Posterior cardinal sinus (deep, entering Duct of Cuvier)
18. Spermatic vein
19. Stomach
20. Testis
21. Thyroid gland
22. Transverse septum
23. Ventricle

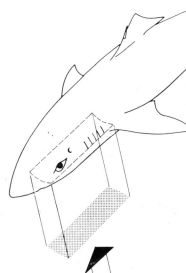

COMMENTS

This photograph shows a posteroventral view with the liver slightly displaced.

The transverse septum divides the coelom of *Squalus* into two major parts, the anterior pericardial and the posterior pleuroperitoneal cavities. These are lined with epithelia that also cover all the viscera, the pericardium and the peritoneum respectively. It is customary to subdivide both into parietal (lining the walls) and visceral (covering contained structures) portions. Since these are very thin epithelia, they are not noted in gross inspection and are not labeled here.

PLATE 15 / 33

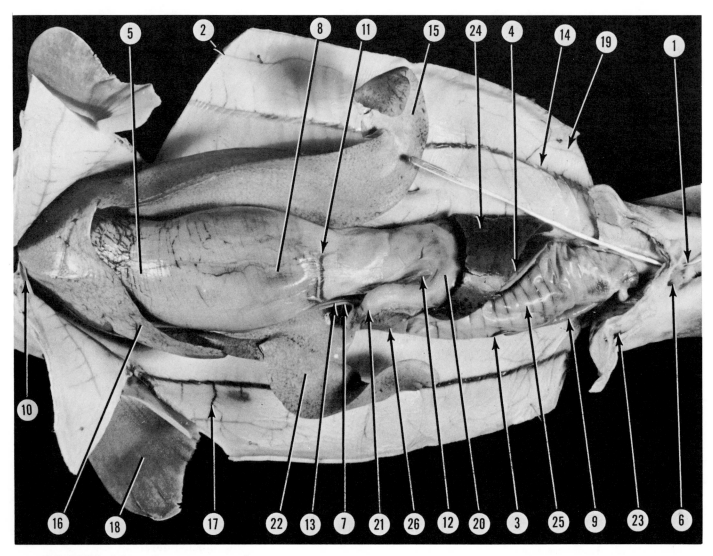

PLATE 16 SITUS VISCERUM—Male

LABELS

1. Abdominal pore with inserted probe
2. Anterior epigastric artery
3. Anterior intestinal artery
4. Anterior mesenteric artery and Posterior intestinal vein
5. Cardiac region of Stomach
6. Cloacal aperture
7. Common bile duct
8. Corpus of Stomach
9. Digitiform gland
10. Falciform ligament
11. Gastric artery and vein
12. Gastrohepatoduodenal ligament
13. Hepatic artery
14. Lateral abdominal vein
15. Left lobe of Liver
16. Median lobe of Liver
17. Parietal vein
18. Pectoral fin
19. Posterior epigastric artery
20. Pyloric region of Stomach
21. Pylorus
22. Right lobe of Liver
23. Siphon (in section)
24. Spleen
25. Valvular intestine
26. Ventral lobe of Pancreas

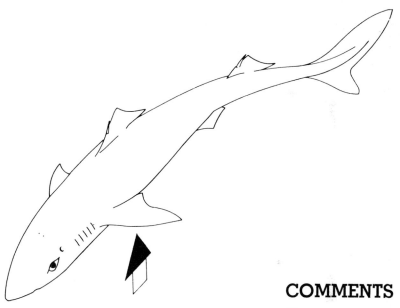

COMMENTS

The filters used show the arteries lighter than the veins.

The left-hand or convex surface of the stomach is generally referred to as the greater curvature, and the right-hand or concave surface as the lesser curvature. The former represents the primitive dorsal surface and to it is attached the mesogaster.

PLATE 16 / 35

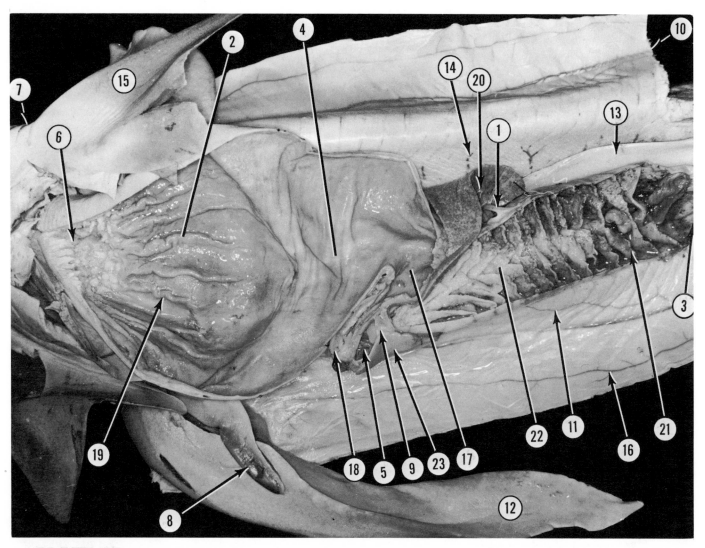

PLATE 17 DIGESTIVE TRACT—Opened view, female

LABELS

1. Anterior mesenteric artery
2. Cardiac region of Stomach
3. Colon
4. Corpus of Stomach
5. Duodenum
6. Esophagus with Papillae
7. External gill slit
8. Gall bladder
9. Isthmus of Pancreas
10. Lateral abdominal vein
11. Lateral artery
12. Liver
13. Oviduct
14. Parietal vein
15. Pectoral fin
16. Posterior epigastric artery
17. Pyloric region of Stomach
18. Pylorus
19. Ruga of Stomach
20. Spleen
21. Spiral valve
22. Valvular intestine
23. Ventral lobe of Pancreas

COMMENTS

The contents of the stomach have been removed. Both the height of the longitudinal ridges or rugae and the thickness of the wall overlying them vary drastically depending on distension (compare Plate 38). There is also a regional difference in the thickness of circumferential muscle, this being greatest in the cardiac and pyloric portions of the stomach.

The valvular intestine was distended with water, deep-frozen, and then dissected in the frozen condition.

PLATE 17 / 37

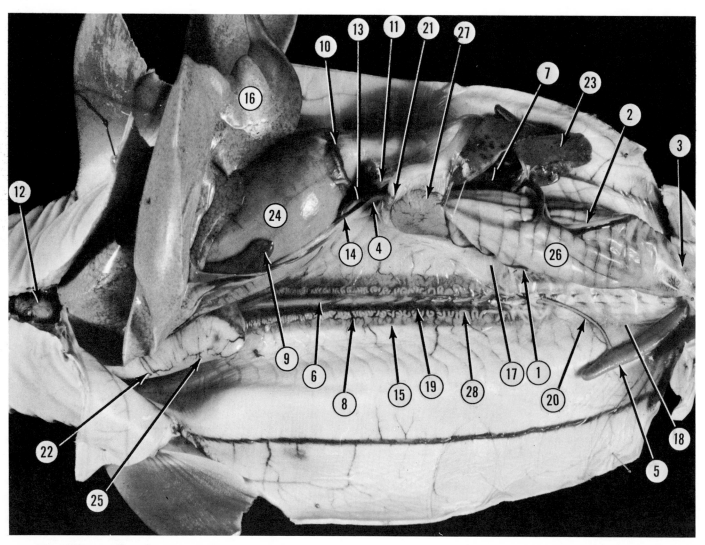

PLATE 18 VISCERA—Male

LABELS

1. Anterior intestinal artery and vein
2. Anterior mesenteric artery and Posterior intestinal vein
3. Colon
4. Common bile duct
5. Digitiform gland
6. Dorsal aorta
7. Dorsal lobe of Pancreas
8. Efferent renal vein
9. Gall bladder
10. Gastric artery and vein
11. Gastrohepatoduodenal ligament
12. Heart
13. Hepatic artery
14. Hepatic portal vein
15. Kidney
16. Liver
17. Mesentery proper
18. Mesorectum
19. Posterior cardinal sinus
20. Posterior mesenteric artery
21. Pylorus
22. Spermatic vein
23. Spleen
24. Stomach
25. Testis
26. Valvular intestine
27. Ventral lobe of Pancreas
28. Wolffian duct

COMMENTS

The digestive tract has been displaced to the left to show the urogenital system.

The male kidney is highly modified. Its anterior portion forms a functional passage between the testis and the Wolffian duct (termed "ductuli efferentia" and "epididymis"). The middle portion of the kidney serves as an accessory reproductive gland (Leydig's gland).

PLATE 18 / 39

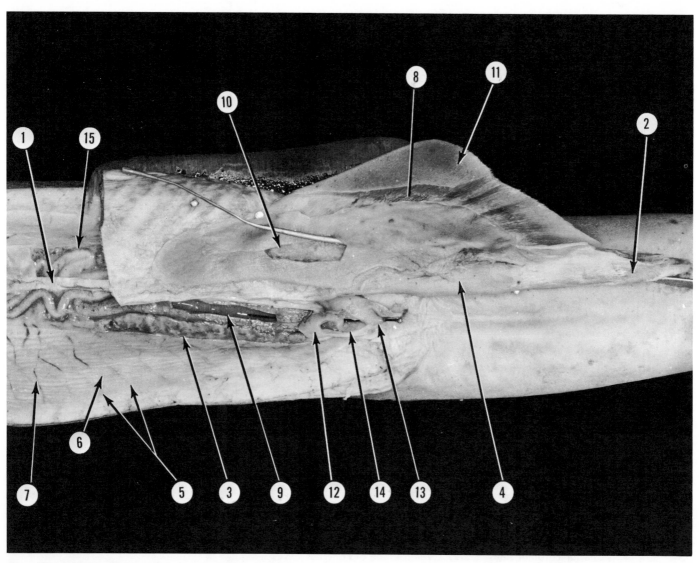

PLATE 19 UROGENITAL DUCTS—Male

LABELS

1. Caudal ligament
2. Clasper
3. Kidney
4. Medial mixipodial muscle
5. Myocommata (internal view)
6. Myomere of Hypaxial musculature
7. Parietal vein (branches)
8. Pelvic fin
9. Seminal vesicle (opened)
10. Siphon (opened with probe in-
    serted and passing out through
    the Spermatic sulcus)
11. Skin
12. Sperm sac
13. Urogenital papilla
14. Urogenital sinus (opened)
15. Wolffian duct

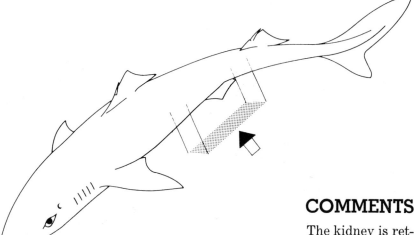

COMMENTS

The kidney is ret-
roperitoneal, lying dorsal to the parietal peritoneum and underlying connective tissue.

The siphon is associated with the
clasper apparatus and presumably
assists in injecting the sperm.

Note the pin which is inserted
through the urogenital aperture and
which reaches the seminal vesicle via
the urogenital sinus (the cavity within the urogenital papilla).

PLATE 19 / 41

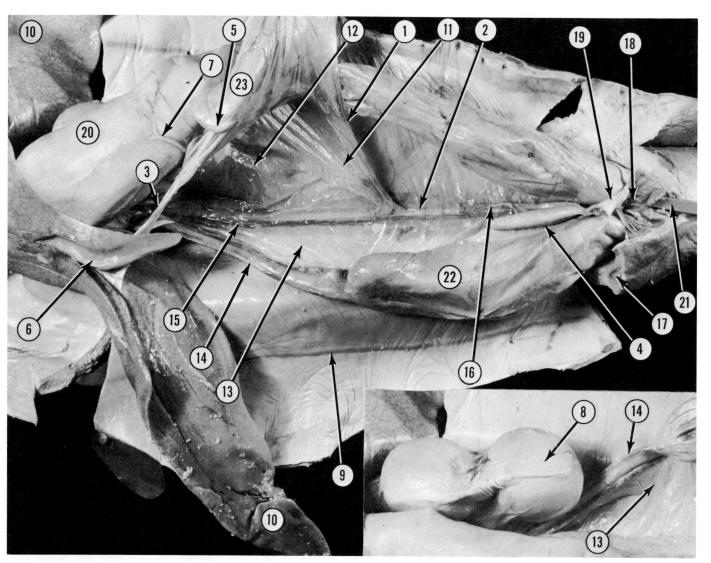

PLATE 20 VISCERA—Female   A. Viscera of female (top left); B. Detail of ripe ovary (bottom right).

LABELS

1. Anterior mesenteric artery
2. Caudal ligament
3. Common bile duct in Gastro-hepatoduodenal ligament
4. Digitiform gland
5. Duodenum
6. Gall bladder
7. Gastric artery and vein
8. Graafian follicle in Ovary
9. Lateral abdominal vein
10. Liver
11. Mesentery proper
12. Mesogaster
13. Mesotubarium
14. Oviduct
15. Posterior cardinal sinus
16. Posterior mesenteric artery
17. Pubo-ischiadic bar (section)
18. Rectocloacal aperture empty-ing into Coprodaeum
19. Rectum
20. Stomach
21. Uterocloacal aperture with probe continuing into Uroda-eum
22. Uterus (distended)
23. Ventral lobe of Pancreas

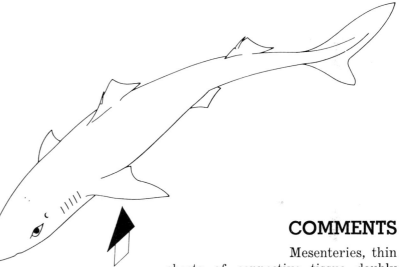

COMMENTS

Mesenteries, thin sheets of connective tissue doubly lined with visceral peritoneum, serve to suspend and orient the viscera. Not shown in this atlas are the mesor-chium which suspends the testis, the mesovarium which suspends the ova-ry, and the gastrosplenic ligament which connects the spleen and stom-ach. The gastrohepatoduodenal liga-ment may be partially subdivided into hepatoduodenal and gastrohepatic lig-aments.

PLATE 20 / 43

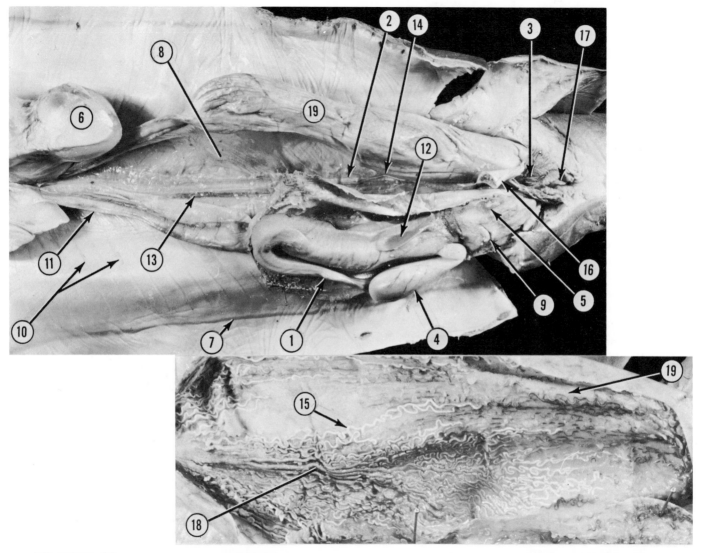

PLATE 21 PREGNANT FEMALE—Details   A. Embryo exposed in urogenital system (top); B. Lining of uterus after removal of embryo (bottom).

LABELS

1. Caudal fin of Embryo
2. Caudal ligament
3. Cloaca
4. External yolk sac with Vitelline arteries
5. Eye of Embryo
6. Graafian follicle in Ovary
7. Lateral abdominal vein
8. Mesotubarium
9. Mouth of Embryo
10. Myocommata (internal view)
11. Oviduct
12. Pectoral fin of Embryo
13. Posterior cardinal sinus
14. Posterior mesenteric artery
15. Posterior oviducal artery (branch of)
16. Rectum
17. Urinary papilla
18. Uterine villi
19. Uterus

COMMENTS

This is the same animal as shown on Plate 20. The right uterus only has been opened to expose the developing embryo (see Scammon, 1911, for description of the growth and development of embryos).

Squalus is considered either viviparous or ovoviviparous by various authors (Hisaw and Albert, 1947). Development may take as long as two years. The prominent arterial branches in the uterine villi certainly serve for respiratory exchange with the uterine fluid; they may also be involved in supplying nutriment to the embryo.

PLATE 21 / 45

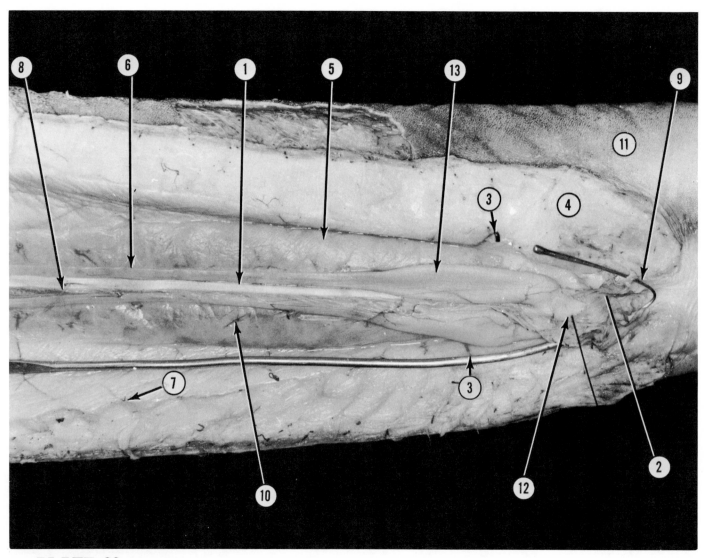

PLATE 22 UROGENITAL DUCTS—Female

LABELS

1. Caudal ligament
2. Cloaca (opened)
3. Iliac artery
4. Hypaxial musculature (cut)
5. Kidney
6. Oviduct
7. Parietal artery (branches in muscles)
8. Posterior mesenteric artery
9. Probe passing through Abdominal pores
10. Renal artery (branch of)
11. Skin
12. Urinary papilla
13. Uterus

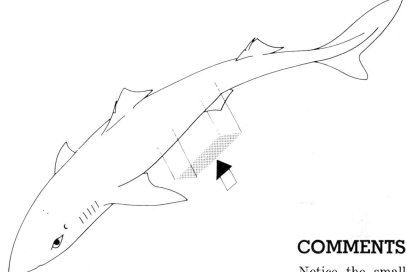

COMMENTS

Notice the small size of the uteri of the nonpregnant female.

Since the uteri open separately into the cloaca, the papilla of the female is urinary only and not urogenital as in the male (see Plate 19). Similarly the female possesses a urinary aperture and a urinary sinus comparable to the urogenital ones in the male.

PLATE 22 / 47

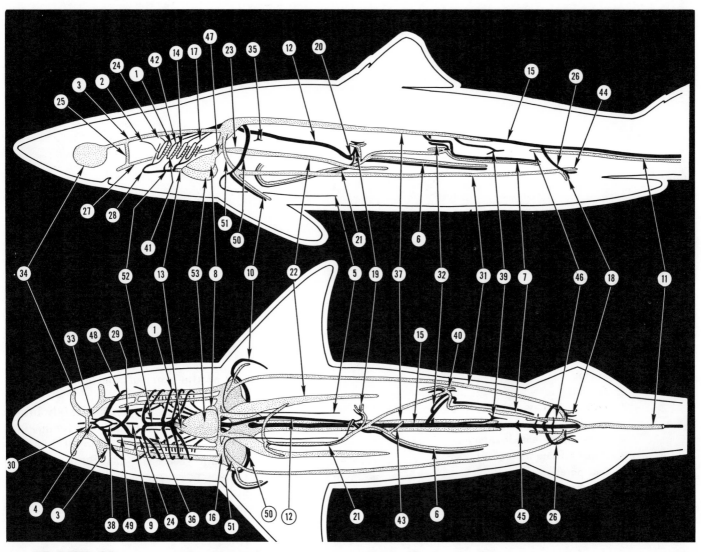

PLATE 23 CIRCULATORY SYSTEM   A. Lateral view (top); B. Ventral view (bottom).

LABELS

1. Afferent branchial artery
2. Afferent spiracular artery
3. Anterior cardinal sinus
4. Anterior cerebral artery
5. Anterior epigastric artery
6. Anterior intestinal artery and vein
7. Anterior mesenteric artery and Posterior intestinal vein
8. Atrium
9. Basilar artery
10. Brachial artery and vein
11. Caudal artery and vein
12. Coeliac artery
13. Conus arteriosus
14. Cross trunks
15. Dorsal aorta
16. Duct of Cuvier
17. Epibranchial artery
18. Femoral artery and vein
19. Gastric artery and vein
20. Gastrohepatic artery
21. Hepatic artery and Hepatic portal vein
22. Hepatic sinus
23. Hepatic vein
24. Hyoidean epibranchial artery
25. Hyoidean sinus
26. Iliac artery
27. Inferior jugular sinus
28. Innominate artery

29. Internal carotid artery
30. Interorbital vein
31. Lateral abdominal vein
32. Lienogastric artery
33. Median cerebral artery
34. Orbital sinus
35. Ovarian or Spermatic artery
36. Paired dorsal aorta
37. Posterior cardinal sinus
38. Posterior cerebral artery
39. Posterior mesenteric artery
40. Posterior splenic vein
41. Post-trematic artery
42. Pretrematic artery
43. Pyloric vein

44. Rectal artery and Cloacal vein
45. Renal artery
46. Renal portal vein
47. Sinus venosus
48. Spiracular epibranchial artery
49. Stapedial artery
50. Subclavian artery
51. Subclavian vein
52. Ventral aorta
53. Ventricle

COMMENTS

These diagrams are intended to tie together the many vessels shown in the photographs. The heart and veins are stippled, the arteries black.

A

B

PLATE 23 / 49

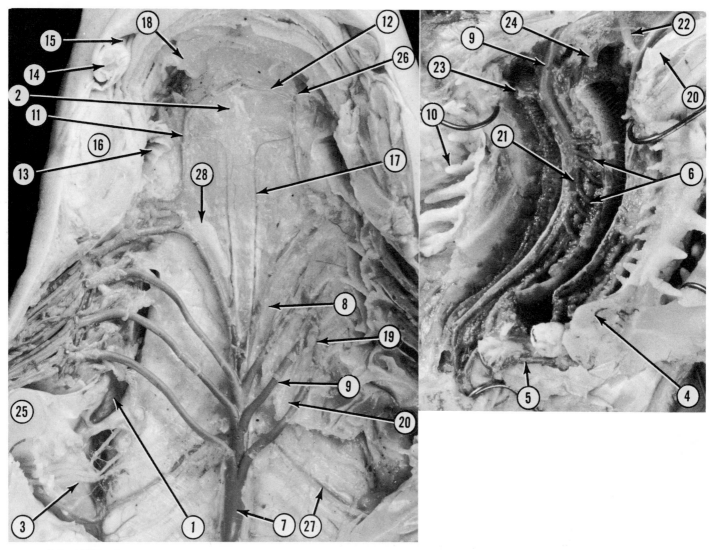

PLATE 24 BRANCHIAL CIRCULATION   A. Efferent branchial circulation in roof of pharynx (left); B. Medial view of right efferent collector loops numbers 2 and 3 (right).

LABELS

1. Anterior cardinal sinus
2. Basal plate of Chondrocranium
3. Brachial plexus
4. Ceratobranchial (ventral end)
5. Commissural artery
6. Cross trunks (anastomoses between Efferent collector loops)
7. Dorsal aorta
8. Dorsal interarcual muscle
9. Epibranchial artery
10. Gill raker
11. Hyoidean epibranchial artery
12. Internal carotid artery
13. Internal spiracular pore
14. Labial cartilage (cut)
15. Labial pocket
16. Mandibular adductor muscle
17. Paired dorsal aorta
18. Palatoquadrate
19. Pharyngeo-esophageal artery
20. Pharyngobranchial
21. Post-trematic artery
22. Post-trematic branch of Vagus nerve
23. Pretrematic artery
24. Pretrematic branch of Vagus nerve
25. Scapular process (cut)
26. Stapedial artery
27. Subclavian artery
28. Subspinal muscle

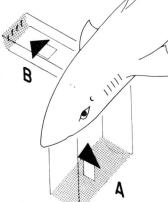

COMMENTS

Although the embryonic epibranchial arteries line up with the branchial bars, they shift position and align with the gill pouches (tremata) in the adult.

In these photographs most of the actual arterial walls have been dissected away and only the latex injection mass remains.

PLATE 24 / 51

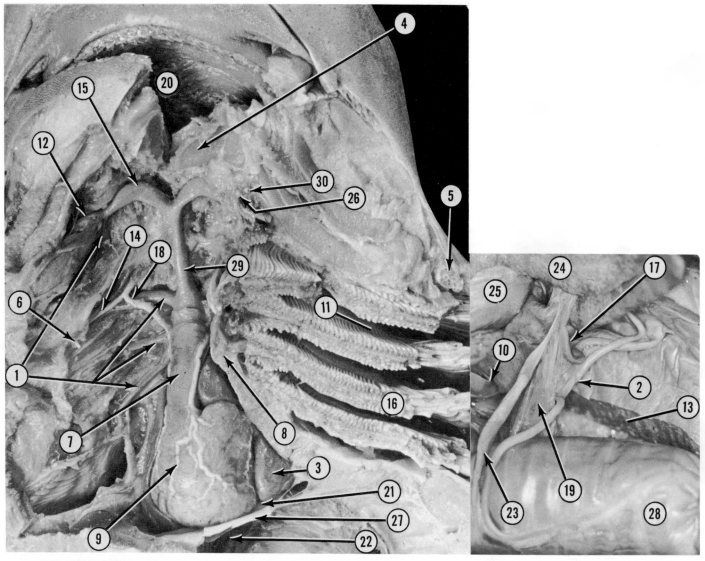

PLATE 25 CIRCULATION—Details A. Ventral view of heart and afferent branchial arteries (left); B. Detail of visceral circulation (right).

LABELS

1. Afferent branchial arteries
2. Anterior mesenteric artery
3. Atrium
4. Basihyal
5. Canals of Lorenzini
6. Commissural artery (stump of)
7. Conus arteriosus
8. Coracobranchial muscle
9. Coronary artery on surface of Ventricle
10. Dorsal lobe of Pancreas
11. Gill pouch
12. Hyoidean afferent branchial artery
13. Hypaxial musculature (cut surface of lateral body wall)
14. Hypobranchial coracoid artery
15. Innominate artery
16. Interbranchial septum between rows of Primary lamellae
17. Lienogastric artery
18. Median hypobranchial artery
19. Mesentery proper
20. Oral cavity
21. Pericardial cavity
22. Pleuroperitoneal cavity
23. Posterior intestinal vein
24. Spleen
25. Stomach
26. Superficial hyoid artery
27. Transverse septum
28. Valvular intestine
29. Ventral aorta
30. Ventral mandibular artery

COMMENTS

In Fig. A only the light-colored vessels are injected. The various hypobranchial arteries vary considerably within this species. The superficial hyoid and the ventral mandibular arteries are the terminal branches of the external carotid.

Figure B shows a ventral view of the major blood vessels lying between the posterior end of the stomach and the anterior end of the valvular intestine. The area shown is that lying between numbers 7, 23, 2, and 26 in Plate 18.

PLATE 25 / 53

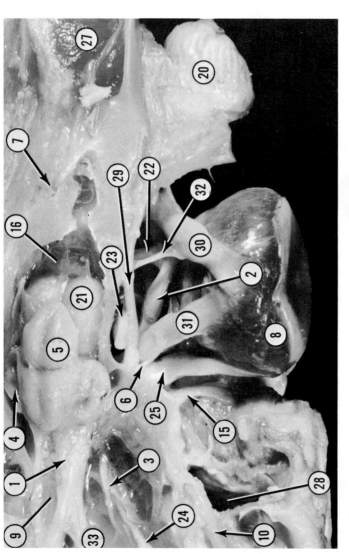

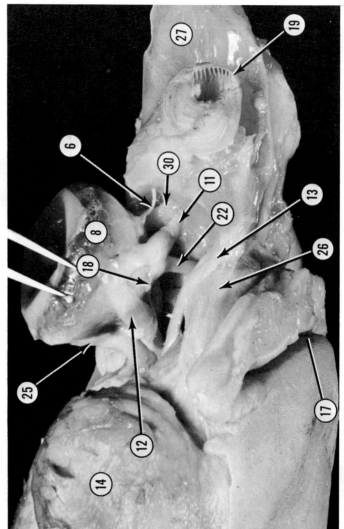

PLATE 26 DISSECTION OF ORBIT   A. Dorsal view (top); B. Ventrolateral view (bottom).

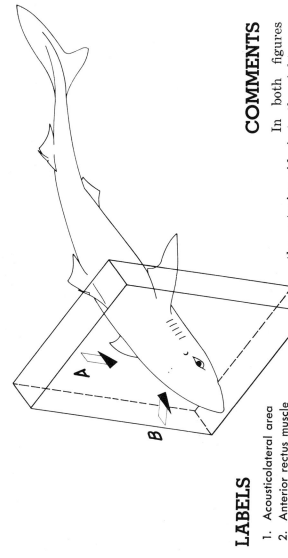

LABELS

1. Acousticolateral area
2. Anterior rectus muscle
3. Auditory nerve
4. Auricle of Cerebellum
5. Body of Cerebellum
6. Deep ophthalmic branch of Trigeminal nerve
7. Epiphyseal foramen
8. Eye
9. Fourth ventricle within Medulla oblongata
10. Hyomandibular trunk of Facial nerve
11. Inferior oblique muscle
12. Inferior rectus muscle
13. Infraorbital trunk
14. Mandibular adductor muscle
15. Mandibular branch of Trigeminal nerve
16. Meninx primitiva
17. Mouth
18. Oculomotor nerve (branch of)
19. Olfactory lamellae within Nasal cavity
20. Olfactory sac
21. Optic lobe
22. Optic nerve
23. Orbital process of Palatoquadrate
24. Petrosal ganglion of Glossopharyngeal nerve
25. Posterior rectus muscle
26. Preorbital muscle
27. Rostrum
28. Spiracle
29. Superficial ophthalmic trunk
30. Superior oblique muscle
31. Superior rectus muscle
32. Trochlear nerve passing through Trochlear foramen
33. Vagus nerve

PLATE 26 / 55

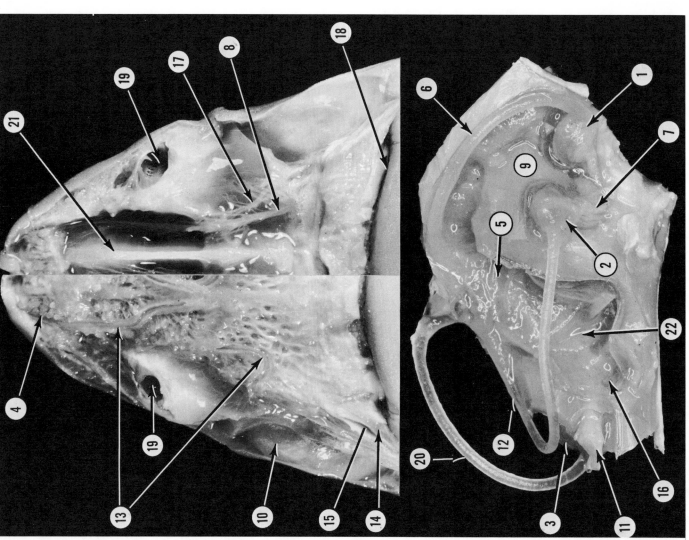

PLATE 27 NEUROMAST SENSORY SYSTEMS A. Ventral dissection of snout, superficial view (top left); B. Ventral dissection of snout, deep view (top right); C. Membranous labyrinth, lateral view of right side (bottom).

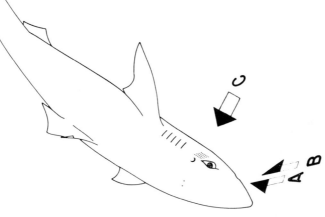

COMMENTS

Figures A and B are trimmed so that the midline is shown on each.

The lateral line system and the otic system share certain histologic characters and both are considered neuromast systems.

The crystalline otolith material lies within the sacculus and is not shown.

LABELS

1. Ampulla of Anterior vertical semicircular canal
2. Ampulla of Horizontal semicircular canal
3. Ampulla of Posterior vertical semicircular canal
4. Ampullae and Canals of Lorenzini
5. Anterior utriculus
6. Anterior vertical semicircular canal
7. Auditory nerve (branch to Crista ampullaris)
8. Buccal branch of Facial nerve
9. Cartilaginous labyrinth
10. Eye
11. Glossopharyngeal nerve (stump of)
12. Horizontal semicircular canal
13. Infraorbital canal
14. Labial cartilage
15. Labial pocket
16. Lagena
17. Maxillary branch of Trigeminal nerve
18. Mouth
19. Nasal cavity
20. Posterior vertical semicircular canal
21. Rostral keel
22. Sacculus

PLATE 27 / 57

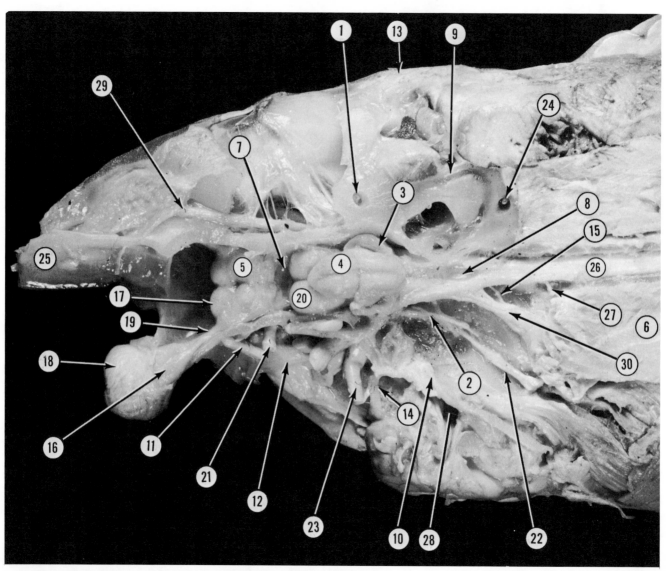

PLATE 28 BRAIN AND CRANIAL NERVES—Dorsal view

LABELS

1. Anterior vertical semicircular canal
2. Auditory nerve in Vestibule of Membranous labyrinth
3. Auricle of Cerebellum
4. Body of Cerebellum
5. Cerebral hemisphere
6. Epibranchial musculature
7. Epithalamus
8. Fourth ventricle within Medulla oblongata
9. Horizontal semicircular canal
10. Hyomandibular trunk of Facial nerve
11. Inferior oblique muscle
12. Infraorbital trunk
13. Mandibular adductor muscle
14. Mandibular branch of Trigeminal nerve
15. Occipital nerve
16. Olfactory bulb in Olfactory foramen
17. Olfactory lobe
18. Olfactory sac
19. Olfactory tract
20. Optic lobe
21. Optic nerve
22. Petrosal ganglion of Glossopharyngeal nerve
23. Posterior rectus muscle
24. Posterior vertical semicircular canal
25. Rostrum
26. Spinal cord within Neural canal of Trunk vertebrae
27. Spinal nerve (number 2)
28. Spiracle
29. Superficial ophthalmic trunk
30. Vagus nerve

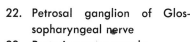

COMMENTS

The right side of the animal has been dissected superficially, the left side deeply.

The right side shows the difference between the cartilaginous labyrinth and the contained and generally smaller membranous labyrinth (see Plate 27).

The primary embryonic differentiation of the brain is into prosencephalon, mesencephalon, and rhombencephalon. The first and last divide in the adult giving the following segments: telencephalon (olfactory apparatus and cerebral hemispheres), diencephalon (epithalamus, thalamus, and hypothalamus), mesencephalon (optic lobes), metencephalon (cerebellum), and myelencephalon (medulla oblongata).

PLATE 28 / 59

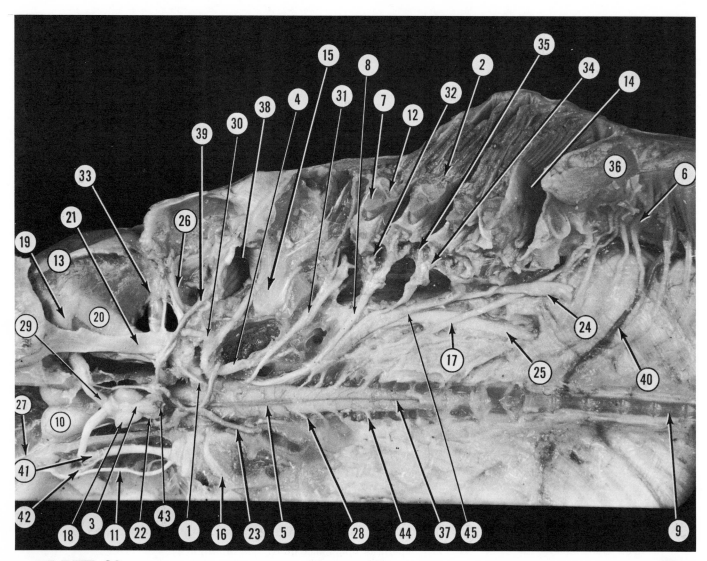

PLATE 29 BRAIN AND CRANIAL NERVES—Ventral view

LABELS

1. Abducens nerve
2. Afferent branchial artery
3. Anterior lobe of Hypophysis
4. Auditory nerve in floor of Vestibule of Membranous labyrinth
5. Basilar artery on surface of Medulla oblongata
6. Brachial plexus
7. Branchial adductor muscle
8. Branchial branch of Vagus nerve
9. Centrum
10. Cerebral hemisphere
11. Deep ophthalmic branch of Trigeminal nerve
12. Epibranchial
13. Eye
14. Gill pouch
15. Hyomandibular (cut)
16. Hyomandibular trunk of Facial nerve
17. Hypobranchial nerve
18. Inferior lobe of Infundibulum
19. Inferior oblique muscle
20. Inferior rectus muscle
21. Infraorbital trunk

22. Intermediate lobe of Hypophysis
23. Internal carotid artery (note the crossing of the two from opposite sides)
24. Intestino-accessory branch of Vagus nerve (cut)
25. Lateral branch of Vagus nerve
26. Mandibular branch of Trigeminal nerve
27. Median cerebral artery
28. Occipital nerve
29. Optic nerves meeting at Optic chiasma

30. Palatine branch of Facial nerve leaving Geniculate ganglion
31. Petrosal ganglion of Glossopharyngeal nerve
32. Pharyngeal branch of Vagus nerve
33. Posterior rectus muscle
34. Post-trematic branch of Vagus nerve
35. Pretrematic branch of Vagus nerve
36. Scapular process (cut)
37. Spinal artery along Ventral fissure of Spinal cord
38. Spiracle
39. Spiracular epibranchial artery
40. Subclavian artery
41. Superficial ophthalmic trunk
42. Trochlear nerve leading to Superior oblique muscle
43. Ventral lobe of Hypophysis
44. Ventral root of Spinal nerve
45. Visceral branch of Vagus nerve

PLATE 29 / 61

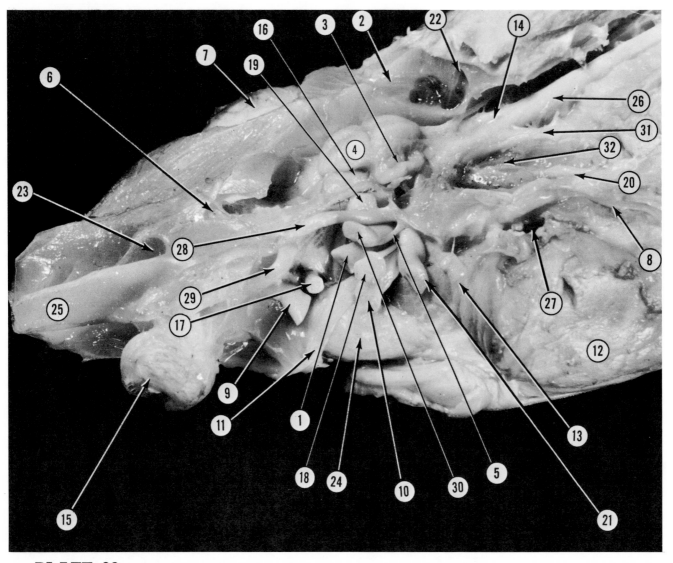

PLATE 30 BRAIN AND ORBIT—Oblique view, dorsolateral and slightly anterior

LABELS

1. Anterior rectus muscle
2. Anterior vertical semicircular canal
3. Auricle of Cerebellum
4. Body of Cerebellum
5. Deep ophthalmic branch of Trigeminal nerve
6. Epiphysis
7. Eye
8. Hyomandibular trunk of Facial nerve
9. Inferior oblique muscle
10. Inferior rectus muscle
11. Infraorbital trunk
12. Mandibular adductor muscle
13. Mandibular branch of Trigeminal nerve
14. Medulla oblongata
15. Olfactory sac
16. Optic lobe
17. Optic nerve
18. Optic pedicel
19. Orbital process of Palatoquadrate
20. Petrosal ganglion
21. Posterior rectus muscle
22. Posterior vertical semicircular canal
23. Precerebral fenestra
24. Preorbital muscle
25. Rostrum
26. Spinal cord
27. Spiracle
28. Superficial ophthalmic trunk
29. Superior oblique muscle
30. Superior rectus muscle
31. Vagus nerve
32. Vestibule of Membranous labyrinth with Otolith

COMMENTS

The central nervous system is hollow. Each part of the brain contains cavities (ventricles). The two lateral ventricles lie in the cerebral hemispheres. The diencephalon surrounds the third ventricle. The cerebral aqueduct of Sylvius and, extending dorsally from it, the optic ventricle lie within the mesencephalon. The metencephalon and myelencephalon contain the cerebellar ventricle and the fourth ventricle respectively. The fourth ventricle is continuous with the central canal of the spinal cord.

PLATE 30 / 63

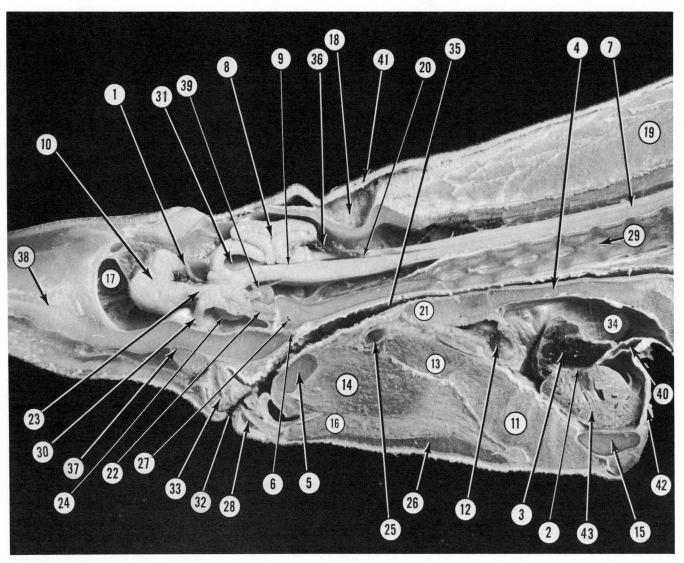

PLATE 31 HEAD—Sagittal section

LABELS

1. Anterior choroid plexus
2. Atrio-ventricular aperture with Atrio-ventricular valve
3. Atrium
4. Basibranchial
5. Basihyal
6. Carotid foramen
7. Central canal in Spinal cord
8. Cerebellar ventricle in Cerebellum
9. Cerebral aqueduct of Sylvius
10. Cerebral hemisphere
11. Common coracoarcual muscle
12. Conus arteriosus at junction with Ventral aorta
13. Coracobranchial muscle
14. Coracohyoid muscle
15. Coracoid bar
16. Coracomandibular muscle
17. Cranial cavity
18. Endolymphatic fossa
19. Epaxial musculature
20. Fourth ventricle within Medulla oblongata
21. Hypobranchial
22. Hypophysis in Sella turcica
23. Hypothalamus
24. Inferior lobe of Infundibulum
25. Innominate artery
26. Intermandibular and Interhyoid muscles
27. Interorbital vein in Interorbital canal
28. Meckel's cartilage with Teeth
29. Notochordal remnant in Trunk vertebra
30. Optic nerve entering Optic chiasma
31. Optic ventricle within Optic lobe
32. Oral cavity
33. Palatoquadrate with Teeth
34. Pericardial cavity
35. Pharynx
36. Posterior choroid plexus
37. Preorbital muscle
38. Rostral keel
39. Saccus vasculosus
40. Sinus venosus
41. Supratemporal canal
42. Transverse septum
43. Ventricle

COMMENTS

There is considerable variation in the terminology used for the parts of the hypophysis; this atlas follows that of Norris (1941).

The aperture in the cranial roof, dorsal to the optic lobes, is an artifact produced in the process of preservation.

PLATE 31 / 65

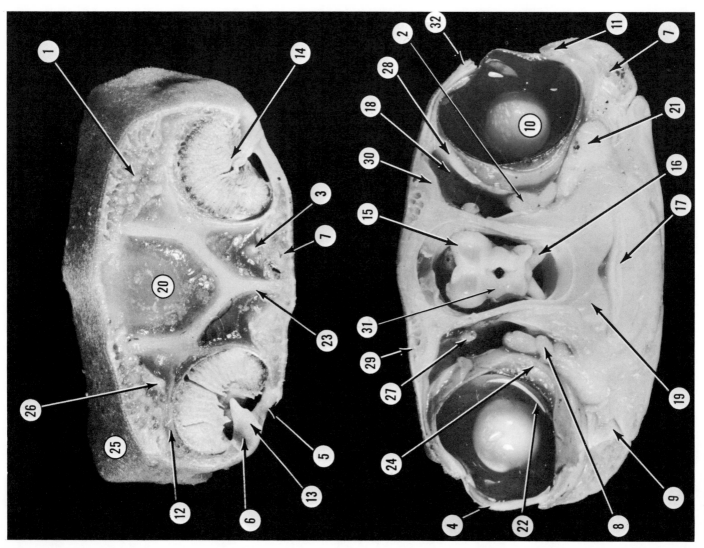

PLATE 32 NOSE AND EYE—Transverse sections A. Section through nasal cavity, anterior view (top); B. Section through eye, posterior view (bottom).

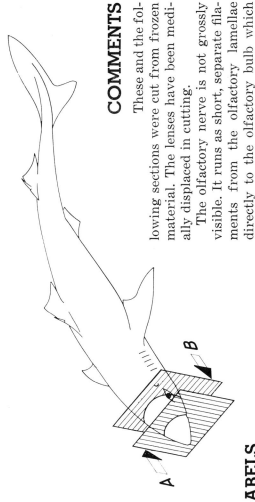

COMMENTS

These and the following sections were cut from frozen material. The lenses have been medially displaced in cutting.

The olfactory nerve is not grossly visible. It runs as short, separate filaments from the olfactory lamellae directly to the olfactory bulb which connects via the olfactory tract to the olfactory lobe. The terminal nerve, which runs along the anteromedial surface of the olfactory tract, is an inconspicuous nerve not usually seen.

LABELS

1. Ampullae and Canals of Lorenzini
2. Anterior rectus muscle
3. Buccal branch of Facial nerve
4. Cornea
5. Excurrent aperture of naris
6. Incurrent aperture of naris
7. Infraorbital cancl
8. Infraorbital trunk
9. Labial pocket
10. Lens
11. Lower eyelid
12. Nasal capsule
13. Nasal flap
14. Olfactory lamellae in Nascl cavity
15. Optic lobe surrounding Optic ventricle
16. Optic nerve entering Optic chiasma
17. Oral cavity (anterior margin of)
18. Orbital sinus
19. Palatoquadrate
20. Precerebral cavity
21. Preorbital muscle
22. Retina and Choroid coat
23. Rostral keel
24. Sclera
25. Skin
26. Superficial ophthalmic branch of Facial nerve
27. Superficial ophthalmic trunk
28. Superior rectus muscle
29. Supraorbital canal
30. Supraorbital crest
31. Thalamus lateral to Third ventricle
32. Upper eyelid

PLATE 32 / 67

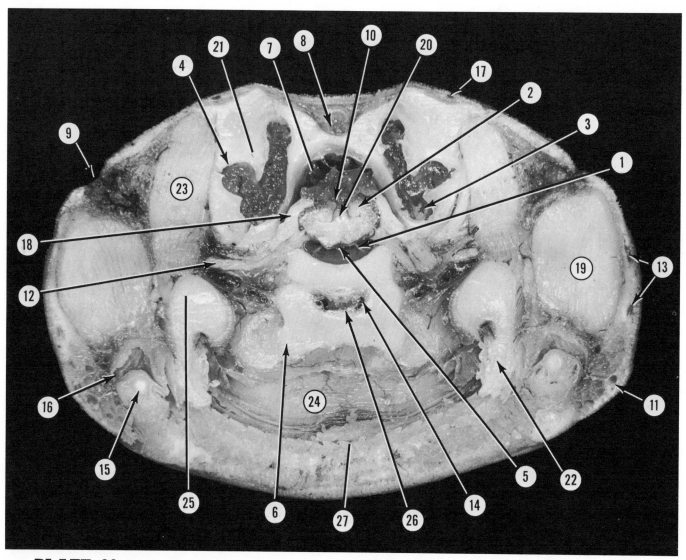

PLATE 33 SPIRACULAR REGION—Transverse section in anterior view

LABELS

1. Abducens nerve
2. Acousticolateral area
3. Ampulla of Anterior vertical semicircular canal
4. Ampulla of Horizontal semicircular canal
5. Basilar artery on ventral surface of Medulla oblongata
6. Basitrabecular process
7. Cranial cavity
8. Endolymphatic fossa
9. External spiracular pore (anterior end of)
10. Fourth ventricle roofed by Posterior choroid plexus
11. Hyomandibular canal
12. Hyomandibular trunk of Facial nerve
13. Infraorbital canal
14. Internal carotid artery
15. Labial cartilage
16. Labial pocket
17. Lateral line canal proper
18. Lateral line root of Facial nerve
19. Mandibular adductor muscle
20. Median sulcus between Somatic motor columns
21. Otic capsule
22. Palatoquadrate with Teeth
23. Palatoquadrate levator muscle
24. Primary tongue in Oral cavity
25. Quadrate region
26. Sella turcica with posterior end of Hypophysis
27. Teeth of lower jaw

COMMENTS

This section is cut at an angle so that the dorsal portion lies posterior to the ventral portion (compare with the sagittal section on Plate 31).

The recognition of quadrate and articular regions of the palatoquadrate and of Meckel's cartilage implies homologies rather than regional differentiation. The terms refer to those portions forming the jaw joint.

The somatic motor column is the most ventral of four such columns, the others, in order, being the visceral motor, visceral sensory, and somatic sensory columns. At this level the somatic sensory column is represented by the acousticolateral area. Sensory and motor areas are separated by the sulcus limitans.

PLATE 33 / 69

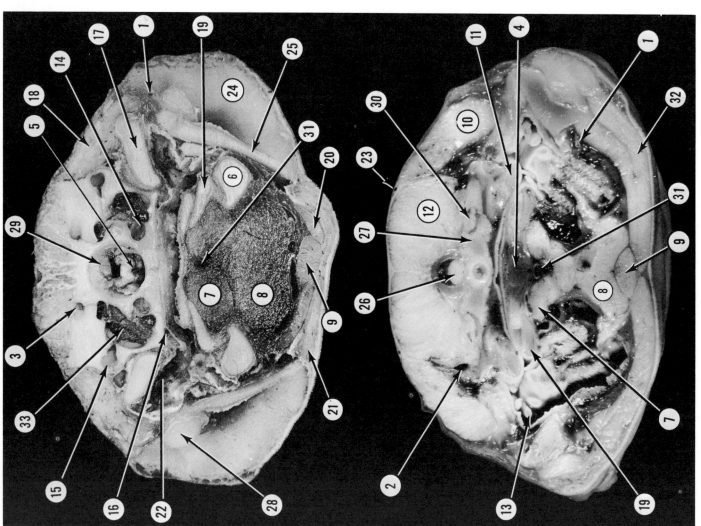

PLATE 34 ANTERIOR PHARYNGEAL REGION—Transverse sections   A. Section through internal spiracular pore, posterior view (top); B. Section through occipital region of chondrocranium, anterior view (bottom).

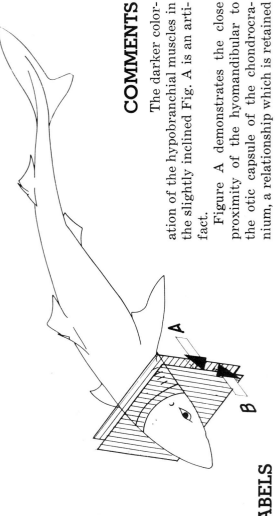

The darker coloration of the hypobranchial muscles in the slightly inclined Fig. A is an artifact.

Figure A demonstrates the close proximity of the hyomandibular to the otic capsule of the chondrocranium, a relationship which is retained in higher forms. Note also that it shows the short region in which the basilar artery is double.

LABELS

1. Afferent spiracular artery
2. Anterior cardinal sinus
3. Anterior vertical semicircular canal
4. Basibranchial
5. Basilar artery on floor of Medulla oblongata
6. Ceratohyal
7. Coracobranchial muscle
8. Coracohyoid muscle
9. Coracomandibular muscle
10. Dorsal hyoid constrictor muscle
11. Epibranchial
12. Epibranchial musculature
13. Gill rakers (in section) in Gill pouch
14. Glossopharyngeal nerve
15. Horizontal semicircular canal
16. Hyoidean epibranchial artery
17. Hyomandibular
18. Hyomandibular levator muscle
19. Hypobranchial
20. Interhyoid muscle
21. Intermandibular muscle
22. Internal spiracular pore
23. Lateral line canal proper
24. Mandibular adductor muscle
25. Meckel's cartilage
26. Medulla oblongata
27. Occipital region of Chondro-cranium
28. Palatoquadrate
29. Posterior choroid plexus in roof of Fourth ventricle
30. Vagus nerve in Vagus foramen
31. Ventral aorta
32. Ventral hyoid constrictor muscle
33. Vestibule of Membranous labyrinth

PLATE 34 / 71

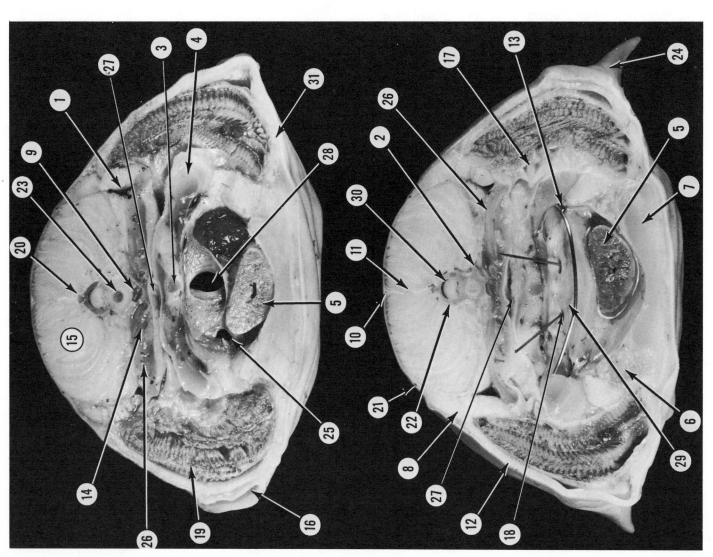

PLATE 35 HEART REGION—Transverse sections   A. Posterior view (top); B. Anterior view (bottom).

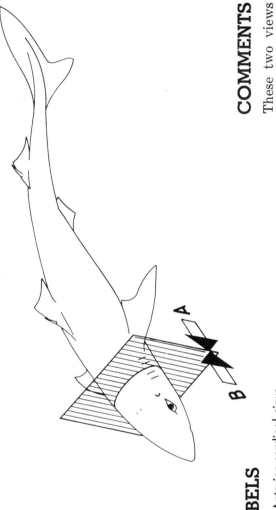

LABELS

1. Anterior cardinal sinus
2. Basapophysis
3. Basibranchial
4. Ceratobranchial
5. Columna carnea in Ventricle
6. Coracobranchial muscle
7. Coracoid bar
8. Cucullaris muscle
9. Dorsal aorta
10. Dorsal cutaneous vein
11. Dorsal skeletogenous septum
12. Dorsal superficial constrictor muscle
13. Duct of Cuvier (with wire)
14. Epibranchial artery
15. Epibranchial musculature
16. External gill slit
17. Gill rakers in Internal gill slit
18. Hepatic vein (with pins)
19. Interbranchial septum between rows of Primary lamellae
20. Interspinous ligament
21. Lateral line canal proper
22. Neural arch
23. Notochordal remnant surrounded by Centrum
24. Pectoral fin
25. Pericardial cavity
26. Pharyngobranchial
27. Pharynx
28. Sinu-atrial aperture with Sinu-atrial valve
29. Sinus venosus (posterior wall)
30. Spinal cord in Neural canal
31. Ventral superficial constrictor muscle

COMMENTS

These two views show a single specimen. The knife cut caused no loss of tissue.

PLATE 35 / 73

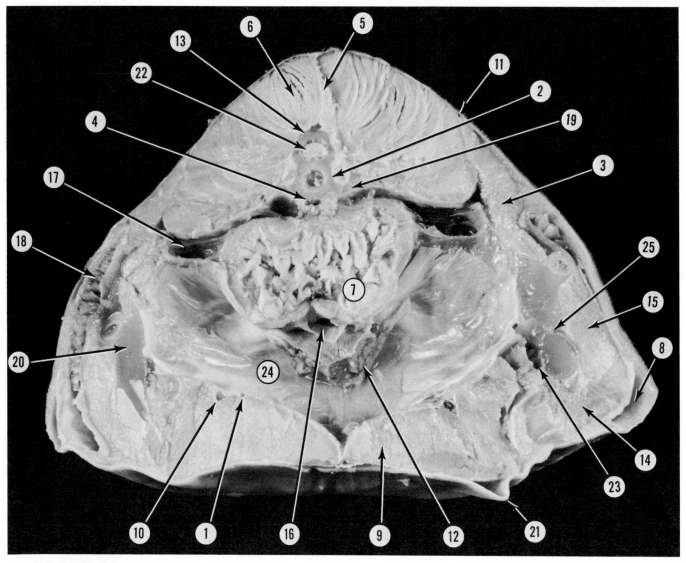

PLATE 36 TRANSVERSE SEPTAL REGION—Transverse section of male in posterior view

LABELS

1. Anterior epigastric artery
2. Centrum enclosing Notochordal remnant
3. Cucullaris muscle
4. Dorsal aorta
5. Dorsal skeletogenous septum
6. Epaxial musculature
7. Esophagus with Papillae
8. External gill slit
9. Hypaxial musculature
10. Lateral abdominal vein
11. Lateral line canal proper
12. Liver (anterior remnant)
13. Neural arch
14. Pectoral depressor muscle
15. Pectoral levator muscle
16. Pericardioperitoneal canal
17. Posterior cardinal sinus
18. Primary lamellae of gill
19. Rib
20. Scapular process
21. Skin (loosened by shrinkage of musculature)
22. Spinal cord in Neural canal
23. Subclavian vein
24. Transverse septum
25. Ventral ramus of Spinal nerve (part of Brachial plexus) in Coracoid foramen

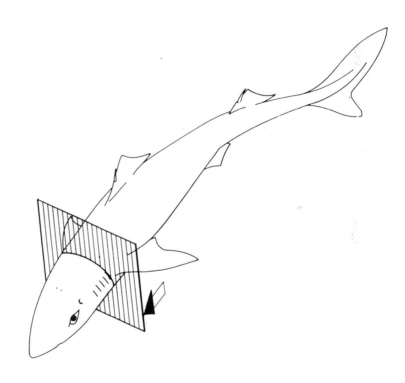

PLATE 36 / 75

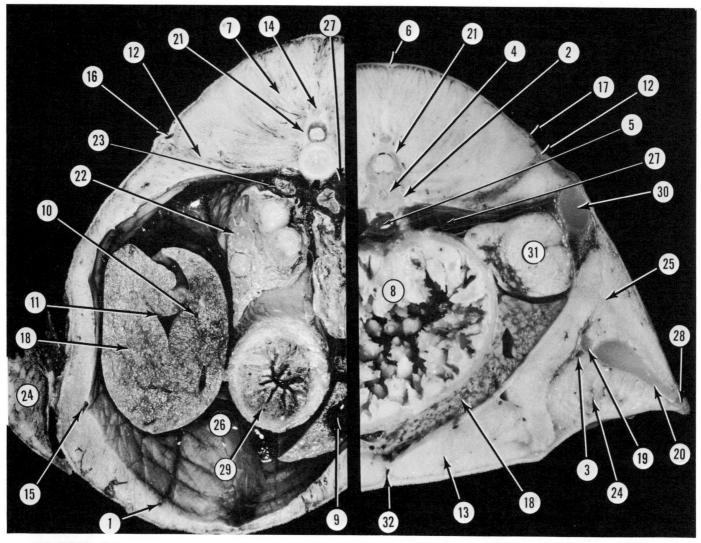

PLATE 37 ANTERIOR TRUNK—Transverse sections   A. Section at level of ovary, posterior view (left); B. Section at level of testis, posterior view (right).

LABELS

1. Anterior epigastric artery
2. Basapophysis
3. Brachial vein
4. Centrum surrounding Noto-chordal remnant
5. Dorsal aorta
6. Dorsal cutaneous vein
7. Epaxial musculature
8. Esophagus with Papillae
9. Gall bladder
10. Hepatic artery (branch of)
11. Hepatic sinus
12. Horizontal skeletogenous sep-tum
13. Hypaxial musculature
14. Interspinous ligament
15. Lateral abdominal vein
16. Lateral cutaneous vein
17. Lateral line canal proper
18. Liver
19. Mesopterygium
20. Metapterygium
21. Neural arch containing Spinal cord in Neural canal
22. Ovary containing Graafian follicles
23. Oviduct
24. Pectoral depressor muscle
25. Pectoral levator muscle
26. Pleuroperitoneal cavity
27. Posterior cardinal sinus
28. Radial pterygiophore
29. Ruga in Cardiac region of Stomach
30. Scapular process
31. Testis
32. Ventral cutaneous vein

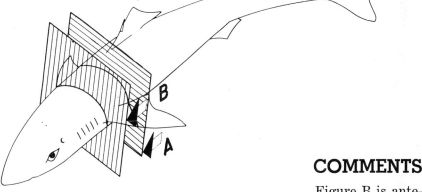

COMMENTS

Figure B is anterior to Fig. A. Note that the liver lobes are fused ventrally at this level.

PLATE 37 / 77

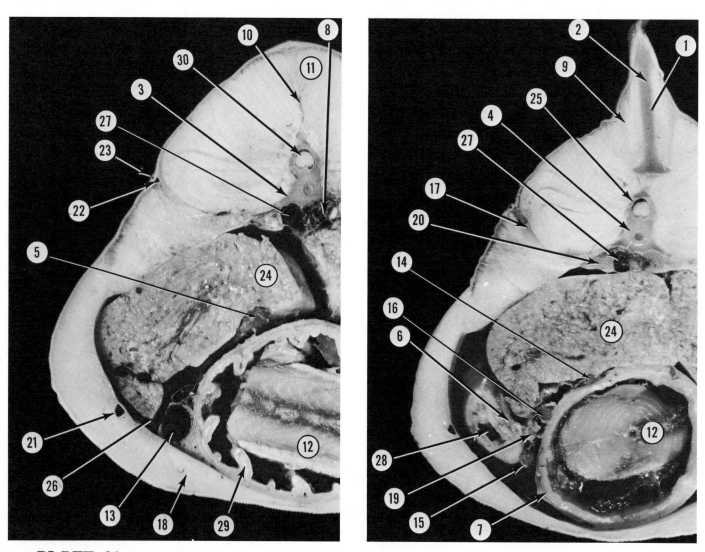

PLATE 38 MIDTRUNK—Transverse sections   A. Stomach region, posterior view of male (left); B. Pyloric region, posterior view of male (right).

LABELS

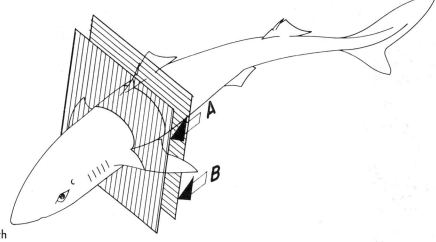

1. Anterior dorsal fin
2. Basal pterygiophore
3. Basapophysis articulating with Rib
4. Centrum surrounding Notochordal remnant
5. Coeliac artery
6. Common bile duct
7. Corpus of Stomach
8. Dorsal aorta
9. Dorsal fin abductor muscle
10. Dorsal skeletogenous septum
11. Epaxial musculature
12. Food in Stomach
13. Gall bladder
14. Gastric vein
15. Gastro-intestinal vein
16. Hepatic portal vein in Gastro-hepatoduodenal ligament

17. Horizontal skeletogenous septum
18. Hypaxial musculature
19. Intestinopyloric artery
20. Kidney
21. Lateral abdominal vein
22. Lateral cutaneous vein
23. Lateral line canal proper
24. Liver
25. Neural arch
26. Pleuroperitoneal cavity
27. Posterior cardinal sinus
28. Pyloric region of Stomach
29. Ruga of Corpus of Stomach
30. Spinal cord in Neural canal

COMMENTS

These pictures demonstrate that sharks swallow chunks of food (bait in this case) without masticating them. The gut is loosely suspended and may shift its position with distension. This accounts for the distorted appearance of captured sharks which have been suspended by the tail.

PLATE 38 / 79

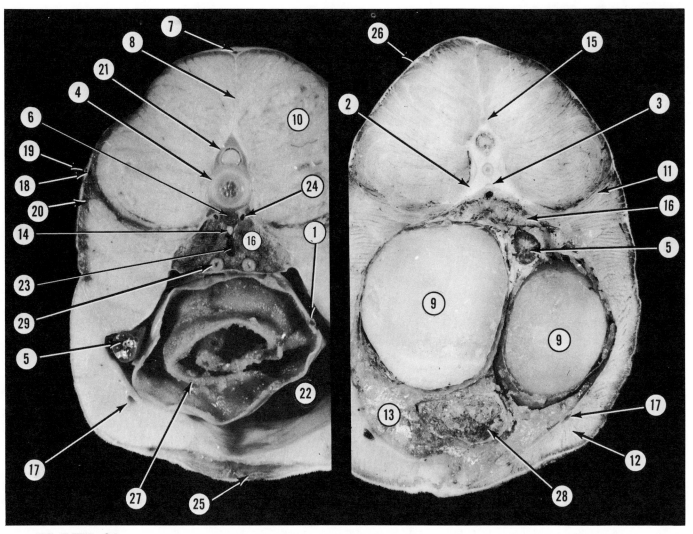

PLATE 39 POSTERIOR TRUNK—Transverse sections   A. Spiral valve of male, posterior view (left); B. Spiral valve region of pregnant female, posterior view (right).

LABELS

1. Anterior mesenteric artery
2. Basapophysis
3. Caudal ligament
4. Centrum surrounding Notochordal remnant
5. Digitiform gland
6. Dorsal aorta
7. Dorsal cutaneous vein
8. Dorsal skeletogenous septum
9. Early embryonic yolk mass filling Uterus
10. Epaxial musculature
11. Horizontal skeletogenous septum
12. Hypaxial musculature
13. Ice filling Pleuroperitoneal cavity
14. Interrenal body
15. Interspinous ligament
16. Kidney
17. Lateral abdominal vein
18. Lateral cutaneous vein
19. Lateral line canal proper
20. Lateral line strip
21. Neural arch enclosing Spinal cord in Neural canal
22. Pleuroperitoneal cavity
23. Posterior cardinal sinus
24. Renal portal vein
25. Siphon
26. Skin
27. Spiral valve in Valvular intestine
28. Valvular intestine
29. Wolffian duct

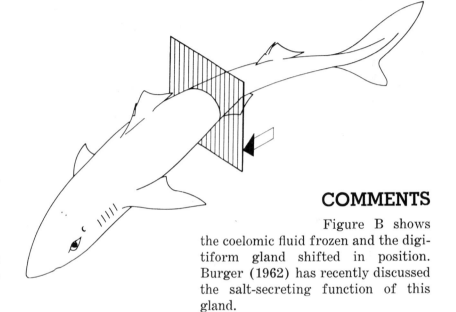

COMMENTS

Figure B shows the coelomic fluid frozen and the digitiform gland shifted in position. Burger (1962) has recently discussed the salt-secreting function of this gland.

PLATE 39 / 81

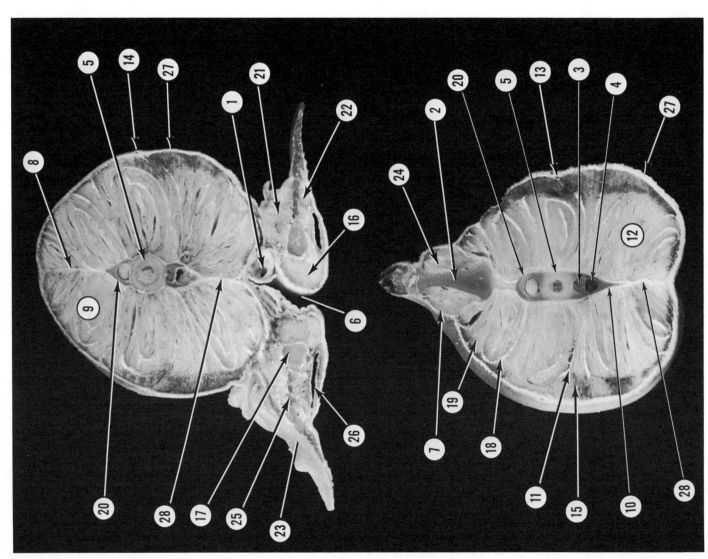

PLATE 40 CLOACA AND TAIL OF MALE—Transverse sections   A. Cloaca of male, anterior view (top); B. Base of posterior dorsal fin, posterior view (bottom).

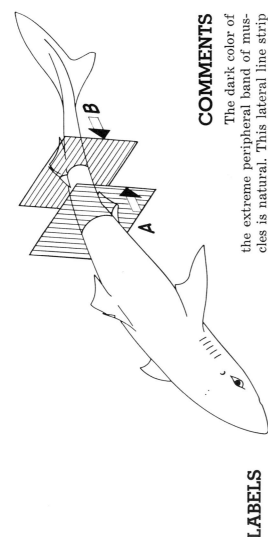

COMMENTS

The dark color of the extreme peripheral band of muscles is natural. This lateral line strip has recently been demonstrated (Boddeke *et al.*, 1959) to be produced by a reduction in muscle fiber diameter and increased vascularization in the dermal attachment zone.

These figures permit a comparison between a caudal vertebra and one of the most posterior of the trunk vertebrae.

LABELS

1. Abdominal pore
2. Basal pterygiophore
3. Caudal artery in Haemal canal
4. Caudal vein in Haemal canal
5. Centrum enclosing Notochordal remnant
6. Cloacal aperture
7. Dorsal fin abductor muscle
8. Dorsal skeletogenous septum
9. Epaxial musculature
10. Haemal spine
11. Horizontal skeletogenous septum
12. Hypaxial musculature
13. Lateral cutaneous vein
14. Lateral line canal proper
15. Lateral line strip
16. Medial mixipodial muscle
17. Metapterygium
18. Myocommata
19. Myomeres
20. Neural arch enclosing Spinal cord in Neural canal

21. Pelvic abductor muscle
22. Pelvic depressor muscle
23. Pelvic fin
24. Posterior dorsal fin
25. Radial pterygiophore
26. Siphon surrounded by Siphon muscle
27. Skin
28. Ventral skeletogenous septum

PLATE 40 / 83

LITERATURE CITED

Bigelow, H. B., and W. C. Schroeder (1948). Sharks. *In* "Fishes of the Western North Atlantic." Vol. 1, pp. 59-576. Sears Foundation Marine Res., New Haven, Connecticut.

Boddeke, R., E. J. Slijper, and A. van der Stelt (1959). Histological characteristics of the body-musculature of fishes in connection with their mode of life. *Koninkl. Ned. Akad. Wetenschap., Proc. Ser. C,* 62: 576-588.

Bolk, L., E. Göppert, E. Kallius, and W. Lubosch (eds.) (1931-1939). "Handbuch der vergleichenden Anatomie der Wirbeltiere." 6 vols. (in 7) plus index. Urban und Schwarzenberg, Berlin and Vienna.

Burger, J. W. (1962). Further studies on the function of the rectal gland in the spiny dogfish. *Physiol. Zool.,* 35: 205-217.

Daniel, J. F. (1934). "The Elasmobranch Fishes." 3rd ed. Univ. of California Press, Berkeley, California.

El-Toubi, M. R. (1949). The development of the chondrocranium of the spiny dogfish, *Acanthias vulgaris (Squalus acanthias).* I. Neurocranium, mandibular and hyoid arches. *J. Morphol.,* 84: 227-279.

El-Toubi, M. R. (1952). The development of the chondrocranium of the spiny dogfish, *Acanthias vulgaris (Squalus acanthias).* II. Branchial arches and extravisceral cartilages. *J. Morphol.,* 90: 33-64.

Grassé, P. P. (ed.) (1958). "Traité de zoologie. Anatomie, Systématique, Biologie." Vol. 13, Pts. 1-3 (Agnathes et Poissons. Anatomie, éthologie, systématique). Masson, Paris.

Hisaw, F. L., and A. Albert (1947). Observations on the reproduction of the spiny dogfish, *Squalus acanthias. Biol. Bull.,* 92: 187-199.

Marinelli, W., and A. Strenger (1959). "Vergleichende Anatomie und Morphologie der Wirbeltiere." Vol. 1, Pt. 3 (*Squalus acanthias*), pp. 173-308. Franz Deuticke, Vienna.

Norris, H. W. (1941). "The plagiostome hypophysis, general morphology and types of structure." Privately published, Grinnell, Iowa.

Norris, H. W., and S. P. Hughes (1920). The cranial, occipital, and anterior spinal nerves of the dogfish, *Squalus acanthias. J. Comp. Neurol.,* 31: 203-402.

O'Donoghue, C. H., and E. B. Abbott (1928). The blood vascular system of the spiny dogfish, *Squalus acanthias* Linné, and *Squalus sucklii* Gill. *Trans. Roy. Soc. Edinburgh,* 55: Pt. 3, pp. 823-890.

Sayles, L. P., and S. G. Hershkowitz (1937). Placoid scale types and their distribution in *Squalus acanthias. Biol. Bull.,* 73: 51-66.

Scammon, R. P. (1911). Normal plates of the development of *Squalus acanthias.* "Normentafeln zur Entwicklung der Wirbeltiere." No. 12.

Willemse, J. J. (1959). The way in which flexures of the body are caused by muscular contractions. *Koninkl. Ned. Akad. Wetenschap., Proc. Ser. C,* 62: 589-593.

Williams, E. E. (1959). Gadow's arcualia and the development of tetrapod vertebrae. *Quart. Rev. Biol.,* 34: 1-32.

INDEX AND SYNONYMY OF ANATOMICAL TERMS

(For a discussion of this Index and its use, see the Introduction.)

Abdominal cavity = Pleuroperitoneal cavity
Abdominal fin = Pelvic fin
Abdominal pore 16-1, 22-9, 40-1
Abdominal vein = Lateral abdominal vein
Abdominal vertebra = Trunk vertebra
Abducens nerve 29-1, 33-1
Acetabular surface 8-1
Acoustic nerve = Auditory nerve
Acousticolateral area 26-1, 33-C, 33-2
Acousticolateral area *also* = Acousticolateral area
    plus Auricle of cerebellum
Actinotrichia = Ceratotrichia
Adductor mandibularis process = Otic process
Adductor muscle of the branchial arch = Branchial
    adductor muscle
Adrenal gland = Interrenal body
Afferent aortic arch = Afferent branchial artery
Afferent branchial artery 10-1, 14-1, 23-1, 25-T,
    25-1, 29-2
Afferent pseudobranchial artery = Afferent spiracu-
    lar artery
Afferent spiracular artery 23-2, 34-1
After brain = Metencephalon
Ampulla of anterior vertical semicircular canal 27-1,
    33-3
Ampulla of ductus deferens = Seminal vesicle
Ampulla of horizontal semicircular canal 27-2, 33-4
Ampulla of Lorenzini 1-12, 27-4, 32-1
Ampulla of posterior vertical semicircular canal
    27-3
Ampullary organ = Ampulla of Lorenzini
Anterior cardinal sinus 23-3, 24-1, 34-2, 35-1
Anterior cardinal vein = Anterior cardinal sinus

Anterior carotid artery = Spiracular epibranchial
    artery
Anterior cerebral artery 23-4
Anterior choroid plexus 31-1
Anterior coronary artery = Coronary artery
Anterior dorsal fin 1-1, 2-1, 7-T, 7-C, 38-1
Anterior efferent branchial artery = Pretrematic
    artery
Anterior efferent-collector = Post-trematic artery
Anterior epigastric artery 15-1, 16-2, 23-5, 36-1, 37-1
Anterior fin = Pectoral fin
Anterior fontanelle = Precerebral fenestra
Anterior gastric vein = Gastric vein
Anterior gastropancreaticosplenic artery = Lienogas-
    tric artery
Anterior intestinal artery 16-3, 18-1, 23-6
Anterior intestinal artery *also* = Anterior intestinal
    plus Intestino-pyloric arteries
Anterior intestinal vein 18-1, 23-6
Anterior intestinal vein *also* = Gastro-intestinal vein
Anterior lateral artery = Anterior epigastric artery
Anterior lobe of hypophysis 29-3
Anterior lobe of hypophysis *also* = *part of* Anterior
    lobe of hypophysis
Anterior median lobe of hypophysis = Anterior lobe
    of hypophysis
Anterior mesenteric artery 16-4, 17-1, 18-2, 20-1,
    23-7, 25-2, 39-1
Anterior mesenteric artery *also* = Anterior intestinal
    artery
Anterior mesenteric vein = Anterior intestinal vein
Anterior oblique semicircular canal = Anterior ver-
    tical semicircular canal

Anterior orbital process = Antorbital process

Anterior part of nasal aperture = Incurrent aperture of naris

Anterior rectus muscle 26-2, 30-1, 32-2

Anterior semicircular canal = Anterior vertical semicircular canal

Anterior semicircular duct = Anterior vertical semicircular canal

Anterior utriculus 27-5

Anterior ventral cutaneous vein = *part of* Ventral cutaneous vein

Anterior ventrolateral artery = Anterior epigastric artery

Anterior vertical semicircular canal 4-1, 27-1, 27-6, 28-1, 30-2, 33-3, 34-3

Antero-dorsal fin = Anterior dorsal fin

Antorbital process 3-1, 4-2

Anus = Cloacal aperture

Anus *also* = Rectocloacal aperture

Aperture of ampulla of Lorenzini = Mucous pore

Aperture of endolymphatic duct = Endolymphatic pore

Aqueduct of brain = Cerebral aqueduct of Sylvius

Aqueduct of Sylvius = Cerebral aqueduct of Sylvius

Archinephric duct = Wolffian duct

Articular process = Glenoid surface

Articular process *also* = Quadrate region

Articular region 33-C

Atrio-ventricular aperture 31-2

Atrioventricular canal = Atrio-ventricular aperture

Atrioventricular orifice = Atrio-ventricular aperture

Atrio-ventricular ostium = Atrio-ventricular aperture

Atrio-ventricular valve 31-2

Atrium 15-2, 23-8, 25-3, 31-3

Auditory capsule = Otic capsule

Auditory nerve 26-3, 27-7, 28-2, 29-4

Auricle = Atrium

Auricle of cerebellum 26-4, 28-3, 30-3

Auricular lobe = Auricle of cerebellum

Auriculo-ventricular aperture = Atrio-ventricular aperture

Auriculo-ventricular valve = Atrio-ventricular valve

Axocranium = Chondrocranium

Basal angle = Basitrabecular process

Basal apophysis = Basapophysis

Basal cartilage = Basal pterygiophore

Basal plate 3-2, 24-2

Basal pterygiophore 7-1, 38-2, 40-2

Basal stump = Basapophysis

Basapophysis 35-2, 37-2, 38-3, 39-2

Basibranchial 5-1, 31-4, 34-4, 35-3

Basi-dorsal = Neural plate

Basihyal 5-2, 25-4, 31-5

Basilar artery 23-9, 29-5, 33-5, 34-C, 34-5

Basipterygium = Basal pterygiophore

Basipterygium *also* = Metapterygium

Basipterygoid process = Basitrabecular process

Basitrabecular process 3-3, 5-3, 12-1, 33-6

Basi-ventral = Haemal plate

Bile duct = Common bile duct

Body of cerebellum 26-5, 28-4, 30-4

Body of stomach = Corpus of stomach

Body of vertebra = Centrum

Body vertebra = Trunk vertebra

Brachial artery 23-10

Brachial plexus 24-3, 29-6, 36-25

Brachial sinus = Brachial vein

Brachial vein 23-10, 37-3

Brain 28-T, 28-C, 29-T, 30-T, 30-C

Branchial adductor muscle 14-2, 29-7

Branchial arch 2-2, 5-C, 14-C

Branchial arch *also* = Branchial bar

Branchial bar 10-C, 14-C, 24-C

Branchial branch of vagus nerve 29-8

Branchial bursa = Gill pouch

Branchial chamber = Gill pouch

Branchial cleft = External *and* Internal gill slits *plus* Gill pouch

Branchial constrictor muscle = Dorsal *and* Ventral superficial constrictor muscles

Branchial lamella = Primary lamella of gill

Branchial levator muscle = Cucullaris muscle

Branchial plica = Gill filament

Branchial pouch = Gill pouch

Branchial ray = Gill ray

Branchiovisceral branch of vagus nerve = Visceral branch of vagus nerve

Buccal branch of facial nerve 27-8, 32-3

Buccal cavity = Oral cavity

Buccal nerve = *part of* Infraorbital trunk

Bulbus cordis = Conus arteriosus

Bursa entiana = Duodenum

Canal of Lorenzini 25-5, 27-4, 32-1

Cardiac aorta = Ventral aorta

Cardiac artery = Coronary artery

Cardiac region of stomach 16-5, 17-C, 17-2, 37-29

Cardiac region of stomach *also* = Cardiac region *plus* Corpus of stomach

Cardinal sinus = *part of* Posterior cardinal sinus

Cardiobranchial plate = Basibranchial

Carotid artery = Hyoidean epibranchial artery

Carotid canal = Carotid foramen

Carotid foramen 3-4, 31-6

Cartilaginous fin ray = Basal *plus* Radial pterygiophores

Cartilaginous labyrinth 27-9, 28-C

Caudal aorta = Caudal artery

Caudal artery 6-C, 6-17, 23-11, 40-3

Caudal fin 1-2, 1-23, 2-3, 7-T, 7-C, 7-5, 7-17, 21-1

Caudal kidney = *part of* Kidney

Caudal ligament 19-1, 20-2, 21-2, 22-1, 39-3

Caudal mesonephros = *part of* Kidney

Caudal opisthonephros = *part of* Kidney

Caudal vein 6-C, 6-18, 23-11, 40-4

Caudal vertebra 2-4, 6-T, 6-C, 6-1, 7-2, 40-C

Caudate lobe of liver = Median lobe of liver

Central canal of spinal cord 30-C, 31-7

Centrum 6-T, 6-2, 29-9, 35-23, 36-2, 37-4, 38-4, 39-4, 40-5

Cephalic kidney = Epididymis *and* Leydig's gland *plus part of* Kidney

Ceratobranchial 5-4, 14-3, 24-4, 35-4

Ceratohyal 5-5, 34-6

Ceratotrichia 7-C, 7-3, 8-2, 11-1, 12-2, 13-1

Cerebellar ventricle 30-C, 31-8

Cerebellum 26-4, 26-5, 28-C, 28-3, 28-4, 30-3, 30-4, 31-8

Cerebral aqueduct of Sylvius 30-C, 31-9

Cerebral artery = *part of* Internal carotid artery

Cerebral cavity = Cranial cavity

Cerebral hemisphere 28-C, 28-5, 29-10, 30-C, 31-10

Cerebral hemisphere *also* = Cerebral hemisphere *plus* Olfactory lobe

Cerebrum = Cerebral hemisphere

Cervical nerve = Hypobranchial nerve

Cervical plexus = Hypobranchial nerve

Cervical rectus muscle = Common coracoarcual *plus* Coracohyoid muscles

Cervicobrachial plexus = Brachial plexus

Chondrocranium 2-5, 3-T, 3-C, 4-C, 11-21, 12-C, 12-3, 24-2, 34-T, 34-C, 34-27

Chondrocranium *also* = Chondrocranium *plus* Splanchnocranium

Chorda dorsalis = Notochordal remnant

Chorda tendinea = Columna carnea

Choroid coat 32-22

Choroid plexus = Anterior *and* Posterior choroid plexus

Choroid plexus of fourth ventricle = Posterior choroid plexus

Choroid plexus of third ventricle = Anterior choroid plexus

Circle of Willis = Anterior *plus* Posterior cerebral arteries

Circulatory system   23-T 24-T, 25-T
Clasper   2-6, 8-C, 8-3, 8-4, 8-11, 19-C, 19-2
Cloaca   6-C, 8-C, 21-3, 22-C, 22-2, 40-T
Cloacal aperture   16-6, 40-6
Cloacal vein   23-44
Coeliac artery   23-12, 38-5
Coeliac axis = Coeliac artery
Coelom   15-C
Collector loop = Efferent collector loop
Colon   17-3, 18-3
Colon *also* = Colon *plus* Rectum
Columna carnea   35-5
Commissural artery   24-5, 25-6
Commissural artery *also* = Commissural *plus* Median hypobranchial arteries
Commissural canal = Supratemporal canal
Common arcual muscle = Common coracoarcual muscle
Common bile duct   16-7, 18-4, 20-3, 38-6
Common cardinal sinus = Duct of Cuvier
Common cardinal vein = Duct of Cuvier
Common carotid artery = Hyoidean epibranchial artery
Common coracoarcual muscle   9-1, 10-2, 31-11
Common hepatic duct = Common bile duct
Conus arteriosus   15-3, 23-13, 25-7, 31-12
Coprodaeum   20-18
Copula = Basibranchial
Copula of hyoid = Basihyal
Copulatory organ = Clasper
Coracoarcual muscle = Common coracoarcual muscle
Coracobranchial muscle   10-3, 25-8, 31-13, 34-7, 35-6
Coracohyoid muscle   10-4, 15-4, 31-14, 34-8
Coracoid = Coracoid bar
Coracoid artery = Anterior epigastric artery
Coracoid bar   7-4, 9-2, 10-5, 15-5, 31-15, 35-7
Coracoid foramen   36-25
Coracoid portion of pectoral girdle = Coracoid bar
Coraco-mandibular artery = External carotid artery

Coracomandibular muscle   10-6, 31-16, 34-9
Corium = *part of* Skin
Cornea   11-14, 32-4
Coronary artery   15-6, 25-9
Coronary artery *also* = Coronary artery *plus* Dorsal pericardial artery (*not shown in Atlas*)
Coronary ligament   15-7
Corpora bigemina = Optic lobes
Corpus calcareum vertebrae   6-3
Corpus of stomach   16-8, 17-4, 38-7, 38-29
Cranial cavity   4-C, 31-17, 33-7
Cranial mesonephros = Epididymis *and* Leydig's gland *plus part of* Kidney
Cranial opisthonephros = Epididymis *and* Leydig's gland *plus part of* Kidney
Cranial pterygial muscle = *part of* Pectoral depressor muscle
Craniomaxillary muscle = Spiracular muscle
Crista = Crista ampullaris
Crista acustica = Crista ampullaris
Crista ampullaris   27-7
Cross connection = Cross trunk
Cross trunk   23-14, 24-6
Crystalline lens = Lens
Cucullaris muscle   11-2, 35-8, 36-3
Cuvierian duct = Duct of Cuvier
Cuvierian sinus = Duct of Cuvier
Cystic lobe of liver = Median lobe of liver
Deep lateral abdominal vein = Lateral abdominal vein
Deep lateral sinus = Lateral abdominal vein
Deep ophthalmic branch of trigeminal nerve   26-6, 29-11, 30-5
Degenerated epibranchial artery = Paired dorsal aorta
Demibranch = Hemibranch
Dermal denticle = Placoid scale
Dermal fin ray = Ceratotrichia
Dermis = *part of* Skin

Dermotrichia = Ceratotrichia

Diacoele = Third ventricle

Diazonal foramen = Coracoid foramen

Diencephalon 28-C, 30-C

Digestive tract 17-T, 18-C

Digitiform gland 16-9, 18-5, 20-4, 39-C, 39-5

Dorsal aorta 18-6, 23-15, 24-7, 35-9, 36-4, 37-5, 38-8, 39-6

Dorsal arcual muscle = Dorsal interarcual muscle

Dorsal arcual muscle *also* = Lateral interarcual muscle

Dorsal branch of segmental artery = Parietal artery

Dorsal branch of vagus nerve = Lateral branch of vagus nerve

Dorsal constrictor muscle = Dorsal superficial constrictor muscle

Dorsal cutaneous vein 35-10, 37-6, 39-7

Dorsal external terminal = Hook of clasper

Dorsal extrabranchial cartilage 4-C, 14-5

Dorsal eyelid = Upper eyelid

Dorsal fin = Anterior *and* Posterior dorsal fins

Dorsal fin abductor muscle 38-9, 40-7

Dorsal hyoid constrictor muscle 11-3, 34-10

Dorsal interarcual muscle 12-C, 12-4, 24-8

Dorsal interarcual muscle *also* = Dorsal interarcual *and* Subspinal muscles

Dorsal intercalary plate 6-C, 6-4

Dorsal intestinal vein = Posterior intestinal vein

Dorsal ligament = Dorsal skeletogenous septum

Dorsal ligament *also* = Interspinous ligament

Dorsal lobe of caudal fin 1-2, 7-C, 7-5

Dorsal lobe of pancreas 18-7, 25-10

Dorsal longitudinal bundle 13-C

Dorsal longitudinal ligament = Interspinous ligament

Dorsal mesentery = Mesentery proper *plus* Mesogaster

Dorsal parietal vein = *part of* Parietal vein

Dorsal pelvic adductor muscle = Pelvic abductor muscle

Dorsal plate = Neural plate

Dorsal pterygial muscle = Pectoral levator muscle

Dorsal root of spinal nerve 6-5

Dorsal septum = Dorsal skeletogenous septum

Dorsal skeletogenous septum 13-2, 35-11, 36-5, 38-10, 39-8, 40-8

Dorsal superficial constrictor muscle 11-4, 12-5, 14-6, 35-12

Dorsal superior constrictor muscle = Dorsal superficial constrictor muscle

Dorso-lateral bundle = Somatic sensory column

Duct of Cuvier 15-17, 23-16, 35-13

Duct of Leydig = *part of* Wolffian duct

Duct of Lorenzini = Canal of Lorenzini

Ductulus efferens 18-C

Ductus choledochus = Common bile duct

Ductus deferens = Wolffian duct

Duodenal vein = Pyloric vein

Duodenohepatic omentum = Hepatoduodenal ligament

Duodenum 17-5, 20-5

Dura mater = Meninx primitiva

Efferent branchial artery = Epibranchial artery

Efferent branchial artery *also* = Pretrematic *and* Post-trematic arteries

Efferent branchial collector artery = Pretrematic *and* Post-trematic arteries

Efferent branchial loop = Efferent collector loop

Efferent collector loop 24-T, 24-6

Efferent hyoidean artery = *first* Pretrematic artery

Efferent pseudobranchial artery = Spiracular epibranchial artery

Efferent renal vein 18-8

Efferent spiracular artery = Spiracular epibranchial artery

Egg = External yolk sac

Eighth cranial nerve = Auditory nerve

First ventral constrictor muscle = Intermandibular muscle

First ventral superior constrictor muscle = Intermandibular muscle

First ventricle = Lateral ventricle

First visceral arch = Mandibular arch

Foetus = Embryo

Foramen for dorsal root of spinal nerve 6-5

Foramen for ventral root of spinal nerve 6-6

Foramen magnum 3-5

Foramen occipitale magnum = Foramen magnum

Forebrain = Prosencephalon

Forebrain *also* = Telencephalon

Fossa rhomboidea = Fourth ventricle

Fourth cranial nerve = Trochlear nerve

Fourth ventricle 26-9, 28-8, 30-C, 31-20, 33-10, 34-29

Fourth ventricle *also* = Cerebellar *plus* Fourth ventricles

Gall bladder 15-8, 17-8, 18-9, 20-6, 37-9, 38-13

Gastric artery 15-9, 16-11, 18-10, 20-7, 23-19

Gastric vein 15-10, 16-11, 18-10, 20-7, 23-19, 38-14

Gastroduodenal vein = Pyloric vein

Gastrohepatic artery 23-20

Gastrohepatic ligament 20-C

Gastrohepatoduodenal ligament 16-12, 18-11, 20-C, 20-3, 38-16

Gastro-intestinal vein 38-15

Gastrolienal ligament = Gastrosplenic ligament

Gastrosplenic artery = Lienogastric artery

Gastrosplenic ligament 20-C

Geniculate ganglion 29-30

Geniocoracoid muscle = Coracomandibular muscle

Geniohyoid muscle = Coracomandibular muscle

Genital artery = Ovarian *or* Spermatic artery

Genital artery *also* = Posterior oviducal artery

Genital pore = Uterocloacal aperture

Genital vein = Spermatic vein *or* Ovarian vein (*not shown in Atlas*)

Gill (*in a general sense*) 9-C, 10-C, 14-T, 14-C, 24-T

Gill *also* = Branchial bar

Gill *also* = Holobranch

Gill arch = Branchial arch

Gill arch *also* = Branchial bar

Gill cartilage = Branchial arch

Gill cleft = External *and* Internal gill slits *plus* Gill pouch

Gill filament 10-C

Gill filament *also* = Primary lamella of gill

Gill lamella = Primary lamella of gill

Gill pocket = Gill pouch

Gill pouch 14-T, 24-C, 25-11, 29-14, 34-13

Gill raker 10-9, 14-9, 24-10, 34-13, 35-17

Gill ray 4-C, 4-7, 5-8, 14-10

Gill septum = Branchial bar

Glandula pterygopodia = Siphon

Glandular part of opisthonephros = Leydig's gland

Glandular sac = Siphon

Glandular sac muscle = Siphon muscle

Glenoid surface 7-6

Glossopharyngeal foramen 3-6

Glossopharyngeal ganglion = Petrosal ganglion

Glossopharyngeal nerve 26-24, 27-11, 28-22, 29-31, 34-14

Graafian follicle 20-8, 21-6, 37-22

Greater curvature of stomach 16-C

Greater omentum = Mesogaster

Groove of clasper = Spermatic sulcus

Gullet = Esophagus

Haemal arch 6-C, 6-7, 7-7

Haemal canal 6-C, 6-8, 40-3, 40-4

Haemal plate 6-C, 6-9

Haemal spine 6-C, 6-10, 40-10

Head 1-C, 11-T, 31-T

Heart 18-12, 23-C, 25-T, 35-T

Hemibranch 10-C

Hepatic artery 16-13, 18-13, 23-21, 37-10

Hepatic channel = *part of* Hepatic sinus
Hepatic portal vein 18-14, 23-21, 38-16
Hepatic sinus 23-22, 37-11
Hepatic sinus *also* = Hepatic sinus *plus* Hepatic vein
Hepatic vein 23-23, 35-18
Hepatic vein *also* = Hepatic sinus *plus* Hepatic vein
Hepatoduodenal ligament 20-C
Hindbrain = Myelencephalon
Hindbrain *also* = Rhombencephalon
Holobranch 10-C
Hook of Clasper 8-4
Horizontal semicircular canal 27-2, 27-12, 28-9, 33-4, 34-15
Horizontal semicircular duct = Horizontal semicircular canal
Horizontal septum = Horizontal skeletogenous septum
Horizontal skeletogenous septum 11-10, 13-C, 13-4, 37-12, 38-17, 39-11, 40-11
Horizontal transverse septum = Horizontal skeletogenous septum
Horny fin ray = Ceratotrichia
Hyoid arch 5-C
Hyoid artery = Superficial hyoid artery
Hyoid branchial ray = Gill ray *of hyoid arch*
Hyoid canal = Hyomandibular canal
Hyoid cartilage = Ceratohyal
Hyoid levator muscle = Hyomandibular levator muscle
Hyoidean afferent branchial artery 25-12
Hyoidean artery = Afferent spiracular *plus* Spiracular epibranchial arteries
Hyoidean artery *also* = Hyoidean epibranchial artery
Hyoidean branch of facial nerve = Hyomandibular trunk of facial nerve
Hyoidean efferent artery = Hyoidean epibranchial artery

Hyoidean efferent collector artery = *first* Pretrematic artery
Hyoidean epibranchial artery 23-24, 24-11, 34-16
Hyoidean sinus 23-25
Hyoidean vein = Hyoidean sinus
Hyomandibular 4-8, 5-9, 29-15, 34-C, 34-17
Hyomandibular artery = External carotid artery
Hyomandibular branch of facial nerve = Hyomandibular trunk of facial nerve
Hyomandibular branch of supraorbital canal = Hyomandibular canal
Hyomandibular canal 33-11
Hyomandibular foramen 3-7
Hyomandibular levator muscle 11-11, 34-18
Hyomandibular ramus = Hyomandibular trunk of facial nerve
Hyomandibular trunk of facial nerve 11-12, 26-10, 28-10, 29-16, 30-8, 33-12
Hypaxial musculature 9-5, 10-10, 11-C, 11-13, 12-9, 13-5, 15-11, 19-6, 22-4, 25-13, 36-9, 37-13, 38-18, 39-12, 40-12
Hypaxonal part of parietal muscles = Hypaxial musculature
Hypobranchial 5-C, 5-10, 31-21, 34-19
Hypobranchial artery = *part of* Commissural artery
Hypobranchial artery *also* = Median hypobranchial artery
Hypobranchial coracoid artery 25-14
Hypobranchial musculature 9-C, 10-T, 34-C
Hypobranchial nerve 29-17
Hypogastric artery = Posterior mesenteric artery
Hypogastric artery *also* = Rectal artery
Hypoglossal musculature = Hypobranchial musculature
Hypoglossal nerve = Hypobranchial nerve
Hypomeric musculature = Hypaxial musculature
Hypophyseal fossa = Sella turcica
Hypophysis 29-3, 29-22, 29-43, 31-C, 31-22, 33-26
Hypophysis cerebri = Hypophysis

Hypothalamus 28-C, 31-23
Ileum = Valvular intestine
Iliac artery 22-3, 23-26
Iliac process 8-5
Iliac vein = Femoral vein
Iliac vein *also* = *posterior end of* Lateral abdominal vein
Incurrent aperture of naris 1-9, 32-6
Incurrent siphon = Incurrent aperture of naris
Inferior jugular sinus 23-27
Inferior lobe of hypophysis = Ventral lobe of hypophysis
Inferior lobe of infundibulum 29-18, 31-24
Inferior lobe of pituitary gland = Inferior lobe of infundibulum
Inferior mesenteric artery = Posterior mesenteric artery
Inferior oblique muscle 26-11, 28-11, 29-19, 30-9
Inferior rectus muscle 26-12, 29-20, 30-10
Infraorbital canal 27-13, 32-7, 33-13
Infraorbital canal *also* = Interorbital canal
Infraorbital trunk 26-13, 28-12, 29-21, 30-11, 32-8
Infundibular stalk = *part of* Infundibulum
Infundibulum 29-18, 31-24
Infundibulum *also* = Infundibulum *plus* Hypophysis
Inner cerebral artery = Anterior cerebral artery
Inner ear = Membranous labyrinth
Innominate artery 23-28, 25-15, 31-25
Innominate ligament = Caudal ligament
Innominate ligament *also* = Interspinous ligament
Integument = Skin
Interarcual muscle = Dorsal *and* Lateral interarcual muscles
Interbasal muscle = Dorsal interarcual muscle
Interbranchial muscle 14-11
Interbranchial septum 14-C, 25-16, 35-19
Interbranchial septum *also* = Branchial bar
Intercalary arch = Dorsal intercalary plate
Intercalary plate = Dorsal intercalary plate

Inter-dorsal = Dorsal intercalary plate
Interhyoid muscle 9-6, 10-11, 31-26, 34-20
Intermandibular muscle 9-7, 10-12, 31-26, 34-21
Intermediate artery = Cross trunk
Intermediate lobe of hypophysis 29-22
Intermediate lobe of hypophysis *also* = *part of* Anterior lobe of hypophysis
Internal branchial aperture = Internal gill slit
Internal branchial fissure = Internal gill slit
Internal carotid artery 23-29, 24-12, 29-23, 33-14
Internal carotid artery *also* = Hyoidean epibranchial *plus* Internal carotid arteries
Internal carotid foramen = Carotid foramen
Internal gill slit 10-13, 14-12, 35-17
Internal jugular vein = Anterior cardinal *plus* Orbital sinuses
Internal rectus muscle = Anterior rectus muscle
Internal spiracular pore 24-13, 34-T, 34-22
Interorbital canal 31-27
Interorbital sinus = Interorbital vein
Interorbital vein 23-30, 31-27
Interrenal body 39-14
Interrenal funiculus = Interrenal body
Inter-renal vein = *part of* Posterior cardinal sinus
Intersegmental artery = Parietal artery
Intersegmental septum = Myocomma
Intersegmental vein = Parietal vein
Interspinous ligament 35-20, 37-14, 39-15
Inter-ventral = Ventral intercalary plate
Intervertebral ligament 6-11
Intervertebral ligament *also* = Interspinous ligament
Intervertebral neural plate = Dorsal intercalary plate
Intestinal artery = Anterior intestinal artery
Intestinal artery *also* = Anterior mesenteric artery
Intestinal artery *also* = Intestinopyloric artery
Intestinal branch of vagus nerve = Intestino-accessory branch of vagus nerve
Intestinal mesentery = Mesentery proper

Intestine = Duodenum *plus* Valvular intestine *plus* Colon *plus* Rectum

Intestino-accessory branch of vagus nerve 12-10, 29-24

Intestinopyloric artery 38-19

Iris 11-14

Iris diaphragm = Iris

Ischio-pubic bar = Pubo-ischiadic bar

Isthmus of pancreas 17-9

Iter = Cerebral aqueduct of Sylvius

Jugular foramen = Vagus foramen

Jugular vein = Anterior cardinal sinus

Jugular vein *also* = Inferior jugular sinus

Kidney 18-C, 18-15, 19-C, 19-3, 22-5, 38-20, 39-16

Labial cartilage 4-9, 5-11, 24-14, 27-14, 33-15

Labial fold 9-8

Labial groove = Labial pocket

Labial pocket 9-9, 10-14, 15-12, 24-15, 27-15, 32-9, 33-16

Lagena 27-16

Large intestine = Colon *plus* Rectum

Lateral abdominal vein 15-13, 16-14, 17-10, 20-9, 21-7, 23-31, 36-10, 37-15, 38-21, 39-17

Lateral artery 17-11

Lateral artery *also* = Anterior epigastric artery

Lateral body = Inferior lobe of infundibulum

Lateral branch of vagus nerve 29-25

Lateral branch of vagus nerve *also* = Visceral branch of vagus nerve

Lateral canal = Lateral line canal proper

Lateral cutaneous vein 37-16, 38-22, 39-18, 40-13

Lateral dorsal aorta = Paired dorsal aorta

Lateral interarcual muscle 12-11

Lateral line 1-10, 13-6

Lateral line branch of vagus nerve = Lateral branch of vagus nerve

Lateral line canal = Lateral line canal proper

Lateral line canal proper 33-17, 34-23, 35-21, 36-11, 37-17, 38-23, 39-19, 40-14

Lateral line foramen = Superficial ophthalmic foramen

Lateral line lobe = Auricle of cerebellum

Lateral line root of facial nerve 33-18

Lateral line septum = Horizontal skeletogenous septum

Lateral line strip of axial musculature 39-20, 40-C, 40-15

Lateral line vein = Lateral cutaneous vein

Lateral lobe of hypophysis = Intermediate lobe of hypophysis

Lateral longitudinal bundle 13-C

Lateral nasal lobe = Nasal flap

Lateral nerve = Lateral branch of vagus nerve

Lateral parietal vein = *part of* Parietal vein

Lateral part of pelvic depressor muscle = Pelvic depressor muscle

Lateral rectus muscle = Posterior rectus muscle

Lateral semicircular canal = Horizontal semicircular canal

Lateral septum = Horizontal skeletogenous septum

Lateral skeletogenous septum = Horizontal skeletogenous septum

Lateral subcutaneous vein = Lateral cutaneous vein

Lateral vein = Lateral abdominal vein

Lateral ventricle 30-C

Left lobe of liver 16-15

Lens 32-C, 32-10

Lesser curvature of stomach 16-C

Lesser omentum = Gastrohepatoduodenal ligament

Leydig's gland 18-C

Lienal artery = Lienogastric artery

Lienogastric artery 23-32, 25-17

Lienogastric ligament = Gastrosplenic ligament

Lienogastric vein = Posterior intestinal vein

Lienomesenteric vein = Posterior intestinal vein

Linea alba 9-10

Linea alba *also* = Horizontal skeletogenous septum

Lip cartilage = Labial cartilage

Liver 15-C, 15-14, 16-15, 16-16, 16-22, 17-12, 18-16, 20-10, 36-12, 37-C, 37-18, 38-24
Lobes of the vagus = Visceral sensory column
Locy's nerve = Terminal nerve
Longitudinal fold of stomach = Ruga of stomach
Lower eyelid 1-11, 32-11
Lower jaw = Meckel's cartilage
Main septum = Horizontal skeletogenous septum
Mandible = Meckel's cartilage
Mandibular adductor muscle 9-11, 10-15, 11-15, 24-16, 26-14, 28-13, 30-12, 33-19, 34-24
Mandibular adductor muscle *also* = Mandibular adductor *plus* Preorbital muscles
Mandibular arch 5-C
Mandibular artery = External carotid artery
Mandibular artery *also* = Ventral mandibular artery
Mandibular branch of trigeminal nerve 26-15, 28-14, 29-26, 30-13
Mandibular cartilage = Meckel's cartilage
Mandibular muscle = Intermandibular muscle
Maxillary branch of trigeminal nerve 27-17
Maxillary levator muscle = Palatoquadrate levator muscle
Maxillary nerve = Infraorbital trunk
Maxillary nerve *also* = Maxillary branch of trigeminal nerve
Meckel's cartilage 2-7, 4-10, 5-12, 9-12, 11-16, 31-28, 33-C, 34-25
Medial arcual muscle = Dorsal interarcual muscle
Medial interarcual muscle = Dorsal interarcual muscle
Medial mixipodial muscle 19-4, 40-16
Medial part of pelvic depressor muscle = Pelvic adductor muscle
Medial rectus muscle = Anterior rectus muscle
Median cerebral artery 23-33, 29-27
Median hypobranchial artery 25-18
Median lobe of liver 16-16
Median longitudinal bundle = Somatic motor column

Median posterior lobe of hypophysis = Ventral lobe of hypophysis
Median sulcus 33-20
Medulla oblongata 26-9, 28-C, 28-8, 29-5, 30-14, 31-20, 33-5, 34-5, 34-26
Medulla spinalis = Spinal cord
Membranous labyrinth 27-T, 28-C, 28-2, 29-4, 30-32, 34-33
Meninx primitiva 26-16
Mesencephalon 28-C, 30-C
Mesencephalon *also* = Optic lobe
Mesentery = Mesentery proper
Mesentery proper 18-17, 20-11, 25-19
Mesocoele = Cerebral aqueduct of Sylvius
Mesocoele *also* = Optic ventricle
Mesocolon = Mesorectum
Mesogaster 16-C, 20-12
Mesohepar = Falciform ligament
Mesointestine = Mesentery proper
Mesonephric duct = Wolffian duct
Mesonephros = Kidney
Mesoophoron = Mesovarium
Mesopterygium 7-8, 37-19
Mesorchium 20-C
Mesorectum 18-18
Mesotubarium 20-13, 21-8
Mesovarium 20-C
Metacoele = Cerebellar ventricle
Metacoele *also* = Fourth ventricle
Metapterygium 7-9, 8-6, 37-20, 40-17
Metencephalon 28-C, 30-C
Metencephalon *also* = Cerebellum
Metencephalon *also* = Myelencephalon
Mid-brain = Mesencephalon
Middle intestine = Duodenum
Middle intestine *also* = Valvular intestine
Mid-ventral cutaneous vein = Ventral cutaneous vein
Mixipodial calcar = Spine of clasper
Mixipodial stria = Spermatic sulcus

Mixipodium = Clasper
Mixipterygium = Clasper
Motor root of spinal nerve = Ventral root of spinal nerve
Motor-oculi nerve = Oculomotor nerve
Mouth 9-13, 10-16, 21-9, 26-17, 27-18
Mouth cavity = Oral cavity
Mucous canal = Canal of Lorenzini
Mucous pore 1-12
Müllerian duct = Oviduct *plus* Uterus
Muscle plate = Myomere
Muscles 9-T, 9-C, 10-T, 11-T, 11-C, 12-T, 12-C, 13-T, 13-C, 14-T
Myelencephalon 28-C, 30-C
Myelencephalon *also* = Medulla oblongata
Myelocoele = Fourth ventricle
Myelon = Spinal cord
Myelonal artery = Spinal artery
Myocomma 9-C, 9-14, 13-C, 13-7, 19-5, 21-10, 40-18
Myomere 13-C, 13-8, 19-6, 40-19
Myoseptum = Dorsal skeletogenous septum
Myoseptum *also* = Myocomma
Myotomal fascia = Subcutaneous fascia
Myotome = Myomere
Narial aperture 5-13
Naris = External naris
Nasal aperture = External naris
Nasal capsule 3-C, 3-8, 4-11, 5-14, 32-12
Nasal capsule *also* = Olfactory sac
Nasal cavity 26-19, 27-19, 32-T, 32-14
Nasal flap 1-13, 32-13
Nasal pit = Olfactory sac
Nasal sac = Olfactory sac
Nerve of the lateral line = Lateral branch of vagus nerve
Nervus terminalis = Terminal nerve
Neural arch 6-C, 6-12, 35-22, 36-13, 37-21, 38-25, 39-21, 40-20
Neural arch *also* = Neural plate

Neural canal 6-13, 28-26, 35-30, 36-22, 37-21, 38-30, 39-21, 40-20
Neural canal *also* = Central canal of spinal cord
Neural plate 6-C, 6-14
Neural process = Neural plate
Neural spine 6-C, 6-15
Neurocoele = Central canal of spinal cord
Neurocranium = Chondrocranium
Neuromast 27-T, 27-C
Ninth cranial nerve = Glossopharyngeal nerve
Nostril = External naris
Nostril *also* = Narial aperture (*of chondrocranium*)
Notochord = Notochordal remnant
Notochordal remnant 6-16, 31-29, 35-23, 36-2, 37-4, 38-4, 39-4, 40-5
Notochordal sheath = *part of* Centrum
Notochordal tissue = Notochordal remnant
Occipital canal = Supratemporal canal
Occipital condyle 3-9
Occipital nerve 28-15, 29-28
Occipital region 34-T, 34-27
Occipito-spinal nerve = Occipital nerve
Oculomotor nerve 26-18
Oesophagus = Esophagus
Olfactory bulb 28-C, 28-16, 32-C
Olfactory capsule = Nasal capsule
Olfactory fila = Olfactory nerve
Olfactory foramen 28-16
Olfactory lamella 26-19, 32-C, 32-14
Olfactory lobe 28-C, 28-17
Olfactory lobe *also* = Cerebral hemisphere *plus* Olfactory lobe
Olfactory lobe *also* = Olfactory bulb
Olfactory lobe *also* = Olfactory bulb *plus* Olfactory tract
Olfactory nerve 32-C
Olfactory peduncle = Olfactory tract
Olfactory pit = Olfactory sac
Olfactory plica = Olfactory lamella

Pectoral adductor muscle = Pectoral depressor muscle

Pectoral depressor muscle   9-15, 36-14, 37-24

Pectoral elevator muscle = Pectoral levator muscle

Pectoral extensor muscle = Pectoral levator muscle

Pectoral fin   1-14, 2-9, 7-T, 9-16, 11-19, 16-18, 17-15, 21-12, 35-24

Pectoral flexor muscle = Pectoral depressor muscle

Pectoral girdle   2-C, 2-10, 7-T

Pectoral levator muscle   11-20, 12-12, 36-15, 37-25

Pectoral plexus = Brachial plexus

Pectoral retractor muscle = Pectoral levator muscle

Pedunculus bulbi = Optic pedicel

Pelvic abductor muscle   13-9, 40-21

Pelvic adductor muscle   12-13

Pelvic adductor muscle *also* = Pelvic adductor *and* Pelvic depressor muscles

Pelvic cartilage = Pelvic girdle

Pelvic depressor muscle   12-14, 40-22

Pelvic depressor muscle *also* = Pelvic adductor *and* Pelvic depressor muscles

Pelvic extensor muscle = Pelvic abductor muscle

Pelvic fin   1-15, 2-11, 8-T, 12-T, 13-10, 19-8, 40-23

Pelvic flexor muscle = Pelvic adductor *and* Pelvic depressor muscles

Pelvic girdle   2-C, 2-12

Pelvic levator muscle = Pelvic abductor muscle

Pelvicobasal muscle = Pelvic adductor muscle

Pericardial cavity   15-C, 25-21, 31-34, 35-25

Pericardial recess = Pericardioperitoneal canal

Pericardioperitoneal canal   36-16

Pericardio-peritoneal septum = Transverse septum

Peritoneal cavity = Pleuroperitoneal cavity

Perivisceral cavity = Pleuroperitoneal cavity

Petrosal ganglion   26-24, 28-22, 29-31, 30-20

Pharyngeal branch of vagus nerve   29-32

Pharyngeo-esophageal artery   24-19

Pharyngobranchial   4-14, 5-21, 12-C, 12-15, 24-20, 35-26

Pharynx   11-T, 24-T, 31-35, 34-T, 35-27

Pia mater = Meninx primitiva

Pineal body = Epiphysis

Pineal stalk = *part of* Epiphysis

Pituitary body = Hypophysis

Pituitary body *also* = Hypophysis *plus* Infundibulum

Pituitary gland = Hypophysis

Placoid scale   1-C, 1-16

Pleural rib = Rib

Pleuroperitoneal cavity   15-C, 25-22, 37-26, 38-26, 39-13, 39-22

Pleuroperitoneum = Parietal *plus* Visceral peritoneum

Plica spiralis = Spiral valve

Pneumogastric foramen = Vagus foramen

Pneumogastric nerve = Vagus nerve

Portal vein = Hepatic portal vein

Postcardinal vein = Posterior cardinal sinus

Posterior cardinal sinus   15-17, 18-19, 20-15, 21-13, 23-37, 36-17, 37-27, 38-27, 39-23

Posterior cardinal vein = Posterior cardinal sinus

Posterior carotid artery = Hyoidean epibranchial *plus* Stapedial arteries

Posterior carotid artery *also* = Paired dorsal aorta

Posterior cerebral artery   23-38

Posterior choroid plexus   31-36, 33-10, 34-29

Posterior communicating artery = Posterior cerebral artery

Posterior dorsal fin   1-17, 2-13, 7-C, 40-T, 40-24

Posterior efferent branchial artery = Post-trematic artery

Posterior efferent-collector = Pretrematic artery

Posterior epigastric artery   16-19, 17-16

Posterior esophageal artery   12-16

Posterior fin = Pelvic fin

Posterior gastric vein = Pyloric vein

Posterior gastropancreaticoduodenal vein = Gastro-intestinal vein

Posterior intestinal artery = *part of* Anterior mesenteric artery

Posterior intestinal vein   16-4, 18-2, 23-7, 25-23

Posterior lienal vein = Posterior splenic vein

Posterior lobe of hypophysis = Intermediate lobe of hypophysis

Posterior lobe of hypophysis *also* = Ventral lobe of hypophysis

Posterior median lobe of hypophysis = *part of* Anterior lobe of hypophysis

Posterior mesenteric artery   18-20, 20-16, 21-14, 22-8, 23-39

Posterior mesenteric vein = Posterior intestinal vein

Posterior oblique semicircular canal = Posterior vertical semicircular canal

Posterior orbital process = Postorbital process

Posterior oviducal artery   21-15

Posterior part of nasal aperture = Excurrent aperture of naris

Posterior peduncle = Auricle of cerebellum

Posterior rectus muscle   26-25, 28-23, 29-33, 30-21

Posterior semicircular canal = Posterior vertical semicircular canal

Posterior semicircular duct = Posterior vertical semicircular canal

Posterior splenic vein   23-40

Posterior ventrolateral artery = Posterior epigastric artery

Posterior vertical semicircular canal   4-15, 27-3, 27-20, 28-24, 30-22

Postero-dorsal fin = Posterior dorsal fin

Postorbital process   3-14, 4-16, 11-21

Postotic fenestra   3-15

Postotic process   3-15

Post-trematic artery   23-41, 24-21

Post-trematic branch of facial nerve = Hyomandibular trunk of facial nerve

Post-trematic branch of vagus nerve   24-22, 29-34

Precerebral cavity   4-C, 32-20

Precerebral fenestra   4-C, 30-23

Pre-olfactory nerve = Terminal nerve

Preorbital muscle   9-C, 12-T, 12-17, 12-23, 26-26, 30-24, 31-37, 32-21

Preorbital process = Antorbital process

Pretrematic artery   23-42, 24-23

Pretrematic branch of vagus nerve   24-24, 29-35

Primary lamella of gill   10-C, 10-17, 14-T, 14-C, 14-13, 25-16, 35-19, 36-18

Primary tongue   33-24

Primary urinary duct = Wolffian duct

Principal lateral septum = Horizontal skeletogenous septum

Principal myoseptum = Horizontal skeletogenous septum

Profundus nerve = Deep ophthalmic branch of trigeminal nerve

Propterygium   7-10, 8-7

Prosencephalon   28-C

Prosencephalon *also* = Telencephalon

Prosocoele = Lateral ventricle

Pseudobranch   1-21, 12-20

Pseudobranchial artery = Afferent spiracular artery

Pterygial nerves = Brachial plexus *plus* Lumbo-sacral plexus (*not shown in Atlas*)

Pterygiophore = Basal *and* Radial pterygiophores

Pterygoquadrate = Palatoquadrate

Puboischiac bar = Pubo-ischiadic bar

Pubo-ischiadic bar   8-8, 12-18, 20-17

Pupil   1-18, 11-22

Pyloric constriction = Pylorus

Pyloric region of stomach   16-20, 17-C, 17-17, 38-T, 38-28

Pyloric sphincter = Pylorus

Pyloric valve = Pylorus

Pyloric vein   23-43

Pylorus   16-21, 17-18, 18-21

Quadrate process = Otic process

Quadrate process *also* = Quadrate region

Quadrate region   33-C, 33-25
Quadratomandibular muscle = Mandibular adductor
   muscle
Radial cartilage = Radial pterygiophore
Radial pterygiophore   7-11, 8-9, 37-28, 40-25
Radix aortae = Paired dorsal aorta
Ramus anastomoticus = Spiracular epibranchial ar-
   tery
Rastiform process = Gill raker
Rectal artery   23-44
Rectal gland = Digitiform gland
Rectal gland artery = Posterior mesenteric artery
Rectocloacal aperture   20-18
Rectum   20-19, 21-16
Rectum also = Colon plus Rectum
Renal artery   22-10, 23-45
Renal portal vein   23-46, 39-24
Renal portal sinus = Renal portal vein
Renal vein = Efferent renal vein
Renal vein also = Renal portal vein
Restiform body = Acousticolateral area
Restiform body also = Acousticolateral area plus
   Auricle of cerebellum
Restiform body also = Auricle of cerebellum
Retina   32-22
Rhinencephalon = Olfactory bulb plus Olfactory
   tract
Rhinencephalon also = Olfactory bulb plus Olfactory
   tract plus Olfactory lobe
Rhinencephalon also = Telencephalon
Rhombencephalon   28-C
Rib   2-14, 36-19, 38-3
Right lobe of liver   16-22
Rostral carina = Rostral keel
Rostral fenestra   3-16, 4-17
Rostral keel   3-17, 27-21, 31-38, 32-23
Rostrum   3-18, 4-C, 4-18, 5-22, 26-27, 28-25, 30-25
Rostrum also = Snout
Ruga of Stomach   17-C, 17-19, 37-29, 38-29

Sacculolith = part of Otolith
Sacculus   27-C, 27-22
Saccus vasculosus   31-39
Scale = Placoid scale
Scapula = Scapular process
Scapular portion = Scapular process
Scapular process   2-10, 7-12, 11-23, 12-19, 24-25, 29-
   36, 36-20, 37-30
Scapular process also = Scapular process plus Šu-
   prascapular cartilage
Scapulo-coracoid = Pectoral girdle minus Supra-
   scapular cartilage
Schneiderian fold = Olfactory lamella
Sclera   32-24
Sclera also = Sclera minus Cornea
Scleroid coat = Sclera
Sclerotic coat = Sclera
Scroll valve = Spiral valve
Second cranial nerve = Optic nerve
Second dorsal constrictor muscle = Dorsal hyoid
   constrictor and Hyomandibular levator muscles
Second dorsal fin = Posterior dorsal fin
Second dorsal superior constrictor muscle = Dorsal
   hyoid constrictor and Hyomandibular levator
   muscles
Second ventral constrictor muscle = Interhyoid and
   Ventral hyoid constrictor muscles
Second ventral superior constrictor muscle = Inter-
   hyoid and Ventral hyoid constrictor muscles
Second ventricle = Lateral ventricle
Second visceral arch = Hyoid arch
Secondary lamella = Gill filament
Segmental artery = Parietal artery
Segmental duct = Wolffian duct
Segmental vein = Parietal vein
Sella turcica   31-22, 33-26
Seminal groove = Spermatic sulcus
Seminal vesicle   19-C, 19-9
Seminal vesicle also = Sperm sac

Sensory fold = Olfactory lamella
Sensory root of spinal nerve = Dorsal root of spinal
   nerve
Serosa = Visceral peritoneum
Seventh cranial nerve = Facial nerve
Short artery = Cross trunk
Shoulder girdle = Pectoral girdle
Sinu-atrial aperture 35-28
Sinuatrial orifice = Sinu-atrial aperture
Sinuatrial ostium = Sinu-atrial aperture
Sinu-atrial valve 35-28
Sinu-auricular aperture = Sinu-atrial aperture
Sinus venosus 23-47, 31-40, 35-29
Siphon 16-23, 19-C, 19-10, 39-25, 40-26
Siphon muscle 40-26
Siphon sac = Siphon
Sixth cranial nerve = Abducens nerve
Skeleton 2-T, 2-C, 4-T, 4-C, 5-T, 7-T
Skin 7-13, 8-10, 11-24, 13-11, 19-11, 22-11, 32-25,
   36-21, 39-26, 40-27
Skull = Chondrocranium *plus* Splanchnocranium
Small intestine = Duodenum *plus* Valvular intestine
Snout 1-19, 27-T
Socket = Orbit
Somactidium = Basal *and* Radial pterygiophores
Somatic motor column 33-C, 33-20
Somatic peritoneum = Parietal peritoneum
Somatic sensory column 33-C
Sperm duct = Wolffian duct
Sperm sac 19-12
Spermary = Testis
Spermatic artery 23-35
Spermatic sulcus 19-10
Spermatic vein 15-18, 18-22
Spinal artery 29-37
Spinal artery *also* = Basilar *plus* Spinal arteries
Spinal canal = Neural canal
Spinal cord 6-19, 28-26, 29-37, 30-C, 30-26, 31-7,
   35-30, 36-22, 37-21, 38-30, 39-21, 40-20

Spinal nerve 6-5, 6-6, 28-27, 29-44, 36-25
Spine of clasper 8-11
Spine of dorsal fin 1-C, 1-20, 2-15, 7-14
Spino-occipital nerve = Occipital nerve
Spino-occipital plexus = Hypobranchial nerve
Spinous process = Neural spine
Spiracle 1-T, 26-28, 28-28, 29-38, 30-27, 33-T
Spiracular artery = Afferent spiracular artery
Spiracular constrictor muscle = Spiracular muscle
Spiracular epibranchial artery 23-48, 29-39
Spiracular muscle 11-25
Spiracular plica = Spiracular valve
Spiracular pseudobranch = Pseudobranch
Spiracular valve 1-21, 12-20
Spiral intestine = Valvular intestine
Spiral valve 17-21, 39-T, 39-27
Spiral valve region of intestine = Valvular intestine
Splanchnic arch = Visceral arch
Splanchnic peritoneum = Visceral peritoneum
Splanchnocranium 4-C
Spleen 16-24, 17-20, 18-23, 20-C, 25-24
Splenic artery = Lienogastric artery
Stalk of epiphysis = *part of* Epiphysis
Stapedial artery 23-49, 24-26
Stomach 15-19, 16-C, 16-5, 16-8, 16-20, 17-C, 17-2,
   17-4, 17-17, 17-19, 18-24, 20-C, 20-20, 25-C, 25-25,
   37-29, 38-T, 38-7, 38-12, 38-28, 38-29
Style of clasper = Spine of clasper
Subcardinal sinus = *part of* Posterior cardinal sinus
Subclavian artery 23-50, 24-27, 29-40
Subclavian vein 23-51, 36-23
Subclavian vein *also* = Brachial vein
Subcutaneous fascia 9-C, 13-C
Subcutaneous stratum = Subcutaneous fascia
Submental artery = Superficial hyoid artery
Suborbital canal = Infraorbital canal
Suborbital muscle = Preorbital muscle
Subspinal muscle 12-C, 12-21, 24-28
Sulcus limitans 33-C

Truncus arteriosus = Ventral aorta
Trunk 1-C, 37-T, 38-T, 39-T
Trunk vertebra 2-16, 4-21, 5-23, 6-T, 6-C, 6-20, 7-16, 28-26, 31-29, 40-C
Tuberculum acusticum = Acousticolateral area
'Tween brain = Diencephalon
Typhlosole = Spiral valve
Upper eyelid 1-22, 32-32
Upper jaw = Palatoquadrate
Urinary aperture 22-C
Urinary orifice = Urinary aperture
Urinary papilla 21-17, 22-C, 22-12
Urinary sinus 22-C
Urinary vesicle = Urinary sinus
Urine duct = Wolffian duct
Urinogenital papilla = Urogenital papilla
Urinogenital sinus = Urogenital sinus
Urodaeum 20-21
Urogenital aperture 19-C, 22-C
Urogenital papilla 19-C, 19-13, 22-C
Urogenital sinus 19-C, 19-14, 22-C
Urogenital system 18-C, 19-T, 19-C, 21-T, 22-T, 22-C
Uterine artery = Posterior oviducal artery
Uterine papilla = Uterine villus
Uterine plica = Uterine villus
Uterine villus 21-C, 21-18
Uterocloacal aperture 20-21
Uterus 20-22, 21-T, 21-C, 21-19, 22-C, 22-13, 39-9
Utriculolith = *part of* Otolith
Utriculus = Anterior utriculus
Vagina = Uterocloacal aperture
Vagus foramen 3-22, 34-30
Vagus nerve 12-10, 24-22, 24-24, 26-33, 28-30, 29-8, 29-24, 29-25, 29-32, 29-34, 29-35, 29-45, 30-31, 34-30
Valve of atrioventricular ostium = Atrio-ventricular valve
Valve of sinuatrial ostium = Sinu-atrial valve

Valvular intestine 16-25, 17-C, 17-22, 18-26, 25-C, 25-28, 39-27, 39-28
Vas efferens = Ductulus efferens
Vena renalis revehens = Efferent renal vein
Vent = Cloacal aperture
Ventral abdominal artery = Anterior epigastric artery
Ventral aorta 23-52, 25-29, 31-12, 34-31
Ventral arch = Haemal arch
Ventral branch of segmental artery = Renal artery
Ventral carotid artery = Afferent spiracular artery
Ventral carotid artery *also* = Spiracular epibranchial artery
Ventral constrictor muscle = Ventral superficial constrictor muscle
Ventral cutaneous vein 37-32
Ventral extrabranchial cartilage 4-C, 14-14
Ventral eyelid = Lower eyelid
Ventral fin = Pelvic fin
Ventral fissure of spinal cord 29-37
Ventral hyoid constrictor muscle 9-17, 34-32
Ventral intercalary plate 6-C, 6-21
Ventral intestinal artery = Anterior intestinal artery
Ventral intestinal vein = Anterior intestinal vein
Ventral lobe of caudal fin 1-23, 7-C, 7-17
Ventral lobe of hypophysis 29-43
Ventral lobe of pancreas 16-26, 17-23, 18-27, 20-23
Ventral longitudinal bundle 13-C
Ventral mandibular artery 25-C, 25-30
Ventral pelvic adductor muscle = Pelvic adductor muscle
Ventral plate = Haemal plate
Ventral pterygial muscle = *part of* Pectoral depressor muscle
Ventral pterygial muscle *also* = Pelvic depressor muscle
Ventral ramus of spinal nerve 36-25
Ventral rib = Rib

Ventral root of spinal nerve 6-6, 29-44
Ventral septum = Ventral skeletogenous septum
Ventral skeletogenous septum 40-28
Ventral spinal artery = Spinal artery
Ventral superficial constrictor muscle 9-18, 10-19, 11-26, 14-15, 35-31
Ventral superior constrictor muscle = Ventral superficial constrictor muscle
Ventricle 15-23, 23-53, 25-9, 31-43, 35-5
Ventriculus = Stomach
Ventro-lateral bundle = Visceral motor column
Vertebra 2-C, 2-4, 2-16, 4-21, 5-23, 6-T, 6-C, 6-1, 6-20, 7-C, 7-2, 7-16, 28-26, 31-29, 40-C
Vertebral artery = Paired dorsal aorta
Vertebral foramen = Neural canal
Vertebral neural plate = Neural plate
Vesicula seminalis = Seminal vesicle
Vestibule of membranous labyrinth 28-2, 29-4, 30-32, 34-33
Vestigial epibranchial artery = Paired dorsal aorta
Viscera 15-T, 15-C, 16-T, 18-T, 20-T, 20-C, 25-T

Visceral arch 5-C
Visceral arch *also* = Branchial arch
Visceral arch *also* = Branchial bar
Visceral branch of vagus nerve 29-45
Visceral branch of vagus nerve *also* = Intestino-accessory branch of vagus nerve
Visceral cleft = External *and* Internal gill slits *plus* Gill pouch
Visceral motor column 33-C
Visceral pericardium 15-C
Visceral peritoneum 15-C, 20-C
Visceral sensory column 33-C
Visceral skeleton = Splanchnocranium
Viscerosensory nucleus = Visceral sensory column
Vitelline artery 21-4
Water sinus = Siphon
Wolffian body = Kidney
Wolffian duct 18-C, 18-28, 19-15, 39-29
Yolk sac = External yolk sac
Yolk stalk = *part of* External yolk sac
Zero cranial nerve = Terminal nerve

5
6
7
8
9
0
1
H 2
I 3
J 4